PRAIS

BREAKTHROUGH LEADERSHIP TEAM

"As our coach for almost 5 years, Mike has helped us to transform our thinking and our ability to perform as a leadership team. By implementing many of the ideas in this book, our business has grown and so has the value we've added to our clients and employees. Read this book with your leadership team and inject these ideas into your company's DNA."

—STEPHANIE HARRIS, CEO OF PARTNERCENTRIC

"As our leadership team coach, I've had a chance to see Mike in action. He has transformed our thinking and ability to perform as leaders and as a team. Many books focus on leadership principles— this book is unique in that it focuses on building, developing, and scaling a great leadership team. This is the most important job for any business leader."

—ALLAN DOW, PRESIDENT OF AMERICAN SOFTWARE

"Heart. Mike. Goldman. These three words go together well. The author has a heart like few leaders I have met in my life's journey...a great heart of giving, service, and value. He is Mike, one of whose meanings is 'gift from God.' Knowing and working with Mike is a gift, he's intense, hilarious, and a master at his craft. The content of Breakthrough Leadership Team will improve lives, leaders, and the profitability of your organization."

—KEITH CUPP, CEO OF GRAVITAS IMPACT PREMIUM COACHES

"Mike understands the challenges and frustrations of business leaders. In simple, easy to use action steps, Breakthrough Leadership Team tackles those challenges and outlines a process that will set the tone for your entire company."

—RYAN SASSON, CEO OF STRATEGIC FINANCIAL SOLUTIONS

"From Mike's decades of experience with leadership teams, he's distilled the key ideas and actions that make those teams tick. This is a book for your entire leadership team. Read it, do it. Then read it again!"

—DAVID ROTH, MANAGING PARTNER OF
RRBB ACCOUNTANTS AND ADVISORS

"Great companies need great leadership teams, and this powerful book explains how to build your team, nurture it, and continuously improve it while your business grows. Read it and then keep it handy for more ideas as your company continues to grow."

—DAVID HERDLINGER, CO-FOUNDER OF KASHBOX COACHING

"Every aspect of company culture and accountability stems from building an effective leadership team. Mike hones in on the vital disciplines every leader must focus on to ensure a successful journey."

—BRUCE ZOLOT, PRESIDENT OF TRAVERS TOOL

Michael,

BREAKTHROUGH LEADERSHIP TEAM

Change your focus,
Change your life!

Will

BREAKTHROUGH LEADERSHIP TEAM

STRENGTHENING
THE HEART
AND SOUL OF
YOUR COMPANY

MIKE GOLDMAN

LIONCREST

PUBLISHING

BREAKTHROUGH LEADERSHIP TEAM

Strengthening the Heart and Soul of Your Company

ISBN   978-1-5445-0740-8 *Hardcover*

       978-1-5445-0738-5 *Paperback*

       978-1-5445-0739-2 *Ebook*

To my amazing wife Angela, for your unending support, encouragement, and love.

CONTENTS

ACKNOWLEDGMENTS

First and foremost, I need to thank my amazing wife, Angela. We took a major risk when I quit my job fifteen years ago to pursue my passion. During our bumpy first few years, when I was ready to give up, she was always there with support and encouragement. The ultimate team player. Thank you for helping me live my dream.

Second, I'd like to thank the many coaches who let me pick their brain for this book: Keith Cupp, Doug Diamond, Jeff Dorman, Sean Evans, Brad Giles, Mark Green, David Herdlinger, Ron Huntington, Kevin Lawrence, Les Rabinovitch, and Shannon Susko.

Lastly, I'd like to thank the many CEOs who agreed to be interviewed for the book: Kevin Comerford, Fred Crosetto, Ben Godsey, David Landsberger, Travis Martin, Mark Nicholson, Todd Perry, Mark Sandridge, Ryan Sasson, David Schnurman, and Andy Warren.

INTRODUCTION

YOU NEED A BREAKTHROUGH
LEADERSHIP TEAM

Think of your company as a human body. If the heart is weak and not pumping blood sufficiently, the body falls apart. Extremities go numb. Organs start to shut down. You can put the patient on dialysis to help the kidneys or use physical therapy to strengthen their arms or legs, but if the blood flow from the heart is sluggish or inconsistent, you can't thrive. The best way to get healthy and feel energetic again is to strengthen the heart.

Your leadership team is the heart of your company.

I've been a business coach and consultant for thirty years and have found that improving leadership teams is the most effective way to bring my clients lasting success.

My core purpose is to help as many people as possible feel fulfilled by their work. I work with leadership teams to create great companies that provide amazing work environments and exciting opportunities for growth. This book provides a framework that will help you develop your own incredible companies and work environments. I wrote this book to not only share my knowledge in helping companies find success, but also to improve the lives of the individuals on leadership teams.

If your leadership team is weak—if its members are overwhelmed, for instance, or not skilled enough to bring fresh ideas that keep your company growing—the problems will spread throughout your organization. If the people on your leadership team aren't working together, the people beneath them won't work together. If the members of your leadership team don't hold themselves accountable, the people who report to them won't hold themselves accountable. If the leadership team is more concerned about individual goals than they are about the team's goals and the company's overarching goals, then the rest of your company will be similarly fractured, and growth and revenue will stall.

Your leadership team isn't just the heart of your company; it's also the soul. A great company with a strong leadership team has a conscience. It's adding value to society. It's solving a problem, addressing a need, or working actively to help its customers do that. Great companies have a sense of purpose that goes beyond profit; they help make the world a better place.

I've learned that the central problem for most struggling companies is their leadership team. As the leadership team goes, so goes the organization. If you don't have a strong leadership team—if you don't have the right people, culture, and processes in place—the company will not grow in a healthy, sustainable way. It will not be the kind of place employees love to work.

Business leaders, too often, focus on the symptoms of problems within their company. Sales are down, so they concentrate on sales. Leads are declining, so they turn their attention to marketing. But if CEOs and other business leaders focused instead on improving their leadership team, they would see ten times the value. More importantly, they would see sustained, long-term value. CEOs can either examine and treat individual organs of their company, or they can work on strengthening the heart—the leadership team—so it can take care of all the other problems at the same time.

Here's what the 2018 Deloitte Global Human Capital Trends Report, a survey of more than 11,000 business and HR leaders, found:

> Fifty-one percent of the respondents we surveyed this year rated "C-suite collaboration" as very important—making it the most important issue in our 2018 survey—and 85 percent said that it was important or very important. Additionally, we found that respondents at organizations with the highest level of CxO cross-collaboration were the most likely to anticipate growth of 10

percent or more. Stunningly, however, 73 percent of respondents told us that their C-suite leaders rarely, if ever, work together on projects or strategic initiatives.

Fifty-four percent of the respondents in our 2018 Global Human Capital Trends survey told us that their companies are not ready, or only somewhat ready, for the level of executive-team collaboration they believe is now required.

Studies also show that the main reason a strategic initiative fails is a lack of leadership buy-in and support (see Figure 1), lending more evidence to the importance of a strong leadership team.

Fig. 1

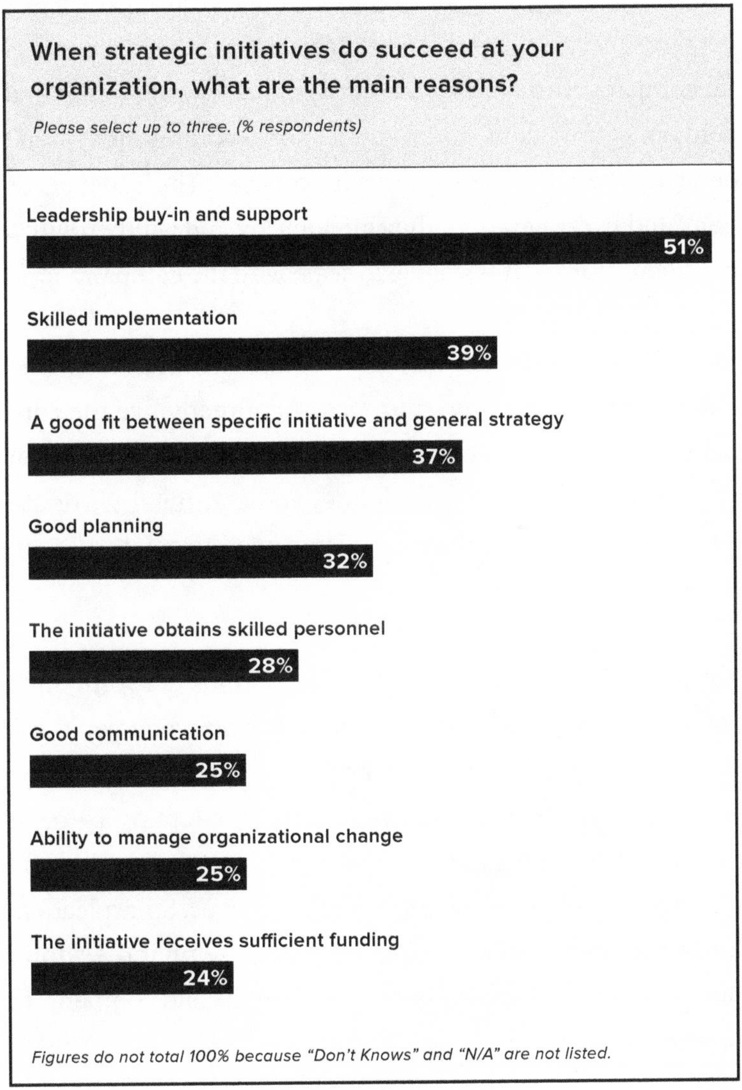

When strategic initiatives do succeed at your organization, what are the main reasons?

Please select up to three. (% respondents)

Leadership buy-in and support
51%

Skilled implementation
39%

A good fit between specific initiative and general strategy
37%

Good planning
32%

The initiative obtains skilled personnel
28%

Good communication
25%

Ability to manage organizational change
25%

The initiative receives sufficient funding
24%

Figures do not total 100% because "Don't Knows" and "N/A" are not listed.

Source: Economist Intelligence Unit Survey, March 2013
© The Economist Intelligence Unit Limited 2013

Leaders with a good business idea think they can white-knuckle it and make things happen. That's how many business leaders become successful in the first place. They launch a successful company through unglamorous, difficult work, but as that company grows, long hours and personal commitment aren't enough to keep the company moving forward. The leader needs help, and in desperation, they hire quickly and wind up with a mediocre team that is unable to scale with the company.

Instead, leaders need to recruit talented individuals who believe in the company's purpose and already live the company's core values. They need to define the culture of their company, execute with discipline, and continually work to develop and improve the team. They need to create a Breakthrough Leadership Team.

Building a Breakthrough Leadership Team is not something you can put on your to-do list and check off when you think you've completed it. Building and shaping the team is a process that never ends. It starts with the CEO adopting a growth mindset, discovering their own strengths and weaknesses, and finding ways to grow and improve themselves. Smart leaders know they can't build a strong leadership team if they don't hire people who complement their strengths and compensate for their weaknesses.

Similarly, you must ensure that the team you assemble has the desire and capacity to learn and grow to meet the needs of the business. Breakthrough Leadership Teams constantly discover new insights they can inject into their DNA to improve the health of the company. Just as a tree can get stronger when it's pruned, leadership teams get stronger when members who aren't up to the task are removed. CEOs must be ready to have those difficult conversations.

Here are some of the other things you'll learn from this book:

- What does a Breakthrough Leadership Team look like, and how do those qualities help create a great company?

- How do you structure your leadership team for success?

- How do you know when to hire for key leadership positions?

- How do you find the right people for your leadership team? What are the proven interviewing and hiring practices?

- How do you create the right culture that cascades down through the rest of the organization? How do you create the right vision and set direction for the leadership team?

- What processes do you need on the leadership team to execute with discipline and accountability and in a way that will improve the performance of the entire company?

- How do you decide when there's a leadership team member

who can't scale with the organization or is holding it back? How do you make and carry out the difficult decision that someone no longer belongs on the team?

- How do you continuously develop and improve as a team? How should your leadership team members continuously develop as individuals?

- Where do you stand on this continuum between having a weak leadership team and having a Breakthrough Leadership Team? How do you spot the gaps and fill in those gaps?

The principles and action plans in this book are based on my decades of experience as a coach and as a business owner. I've also conducted dozens of interviews with leading business coaches and CEOs as I've pulled together the ideas in this book. The practices I describe have proven successful time and again, both in my work coaching companies and in the organizations I've researched. I've implemented the same strategies with companies of all sizes from several industries, and in every case, the companies that committed to strengthening their leadership team went on to enjoy long-term success.

This book was written for CEOs and business leaders who are beginning to build a leadership team. It's also for those who have weak leadership teams they'd like to strengthen, as well as those who have a thriving leadership team and are looking for new ideas to take the team to the next level. It's for CEOs and leaders who want top-line growth, bottom-line growth, and a more fulfilling environment for themselves and their team.

HOW TO USE THIS BOOK

This book is a detailed guide to help CEOs, leaders, and their direct reports build a Breakthrough Leadership Team and ensure that it is continuously improving.

This is not a book about leadership concepts for you to ponder, nor is it a philosophical book about how to become a great leader.

This book outlines specific, practical actions to build and maintain a Breakthrough Leadership Team with an outstanding culture that filters down throughout your company. It provides pragmatic steps to help you become more self-aware and to use that awareness to improve your team and your company. A central principle of this book is that Breakthrough Leadership Teams build companies that not only have regular top- and bottom-line growth but are also great places to work. Employees are fulfilled by their work every day because they are growing and adding value to society.

Each chapter is structured as follows:

- I'll introduce the central theme with an anecdote or story that illustrates a specific challenge and resulting opportunity for the leadership team.

- I'll describe what you should look for to determine the magnitude of the problem or opportunity for your specific leadership team.

- Finally, I'll map out powerful action steps you can take to build your Breakthrough Leadership Team.

To get the most from this book, note areas where you or your company need help and then highlight the action steps that make sense. Finally, take the assessment at the end of the book to help you identify additional opportunities.

Then have your leadership team read the book and take the assessment. Discuss the results as a group and prioritize the key actions you want to take. Follow this process each quarter: take the assessment again and then prioritize your actions. Ask your team this question: What are the one or two areas we need to focus on to improve our leadership team over the next ninety days?

Making this an ongoing process is critical. You'll never get to the perfect state, but following the process helps ensure your leadership team grows as your company grows. Remember, the challenges you face as a $5 million company are much different from challenges you'll face at $50 million or $150 million. This book will help you prepare for those future challenges.

After you and your leadership team have read the book, keep

it handy as a reference. For instance, if you want to fine-tune your hiring process, reread Chapter 3, "Finding the Right People." Worried about your own growth as the leader? Go back to Chapter 1, "Self-Leadership." Worried that your team isn't having productive conflict or is spending too much time blaming instead of working together? Go back and read Chapter 4, "Defining the Right Culture."

MY CHALLENGE FOR YOU

There's always an opportunity to improve, but it requires your full commitment and the full commitment of your leadership team. You and your leadership team must make the team your highest priority. You must commit to continuous learning and to having difficult conversations with each other when you are not aligned. You must commit to achieving your goals as well as to holding fellow teammates accountable.

The process of building a great team starts with self-awareness, so read on to learn what skills and mindset you'll need to build your own Breakthrough Leadership Team—a team that drives top- and bottom-line growth, fosters employee fulfillment, and adds great value to society.

CHAPTER 1

SELF-LEADERSHIP

I got home from work one evening and immediately heard my wife calling for my twelve-year-old son, Richie, to come upstairs for dinner. I could tell from her voice that this was not the first time she'd called him. I glanced down to the den and could see Richie focused on a video game. I sighed.

Richie has Asperger's syndrome, which means that he struggles with social interaction and communication. In his younger years, he had his good days and his bad days, and on his bad days, we all had a hard time. At school, kids would make fun of him, and he'd respond by crawling under his desk. We got a lot of calls from his school. At home, we struggled to get him to do simple things, like put on his shoes or take a shower or come upstairs when dinner was ready. For as much as we loved him, living with him was often stressful and frustrating. How was he going to handle high school? What would happen when he became an adult?

On this occasion, I came home in a bad mood. I had a stressful day, and when I walked through the front door and heard yelling, my anger erupted. I strode down to the den and started screaming at Richie to get upstairs. He shouted back at me, saying that he needed to get to a save point in his video game. I said I didn't care, and then I walked over and did something you should never do to a twelve-year-old with Asperger's playing a video game: I pulled the plug.

Richie began screaming and crying, I screamed back, and when we finally got to the dinner table, my wife and daughter sat there looking at the two of us like we were nuts. We all had a horrible dinner. We barely said a word. It went on to be a horrible night and then a horrible week.

The next week, I had my regularly scheduled session with my business coach Susan. She asked if I'd accomplished the two or three things I'd agreed to do during our last call.

"Don't even go there," I said. "I had a terrible week with Richie. I got almost nothing done." I went on to explain the fight I'd had with Richie and the lousy week I'd had as a result.

Susan listened quietly, then asked, "Mike, what do you think you did to cause that bad week?"

I froze for a second and then took a breath.

"Susan, I didn't cause Richie's *Asperger's!*"

"I know. But is that the first time your son has ever refused to get off the video game or ignored calls to dinner? Does that always lead to a horrible week?" she asked.

I thought back to a time just a few weeks prior. I came home to a very similar situation—Richie playing a game, Angela calling him to dinner. The only difference was that I was in a good mood. I'd had a great day at work, and I came home upbeat and optimistic.

"Hey Richie," I said that night. "Five minutes and then you're upstairs for dinner, okay?"

"Okay," he said.

He came up a few minutes later. No yelling, no recriminations. We had a nice dinner. We had a nice night. We had a happy week.

As I went through these thoughts during my call with Susan, it dawned on me how much influence I have on my family and its happiness. How many times had I come home after a frustrating day and lost patience with my son? How many times had I come home thinking, *Why doesn't this kid just act like other kids?* On a good day, my attitude would be, *Hey, this kid is having a tough time, but he's doing the best he can. How can I be the best dad I can be? How can I help him? How can I support him?* Why hadn't I learned to maintain this attitude and practice these behaviors so we could have good weeks rather than bad ones? I can't cure my son's Asperger's, but I can change how I behave and focus on what I can control, and in that process create a much better way for all of us.

ATTITUDE AND EMOTIONAL CONTROL

I tell this story because it illustrates how leaders must acknowledge that their behavior can have a profound effect—both good and bad—on their company, their leadership team, and their families. As the leader, if you are not growing and improving, then your organization is not growing and improving. If you don't have the attitude and emotional control of a great leader, you limit your effectiveness with your team and the company.

In his book *The 21 Irrefutable Laws of Leadership*, John Maxwell describes what he calls "the law of the lid."

"Your leadership ability—for better or for worse—always determines your effectiveness and the potential impact of your organization," Maxwell says. Your team will never scale faster than your ability to scale as a leader.

The law of the lid underscores the value of putting time and effort into self-improvement. That means reading books, attending conferences, or getting a business coach, but it also means understanding yourself, nurturing your confidence, hiring people who are strong in areas where you are weak, and developing the behaviors and practices that give you a sturdy emotional keel and keep you on course.

It sounds challenging, and it is. Sometimes, like when I realized with the help of my coach that I wasn't consistently behaving like father of the year with my son, it can be sobering. But at the same time, the effects can be tremendously liberating for you and your company—providing you adopt the right mindset and follow through on your good intentions.

SYMPTOMS OF POOR SELF-LEADERSHIP

I specialize in working with leadership teams, but I also make it a requirement that I work with the CEO in a one-on-one capacity. I've learned that if the leader is not actively engaged in polishing or expanding their self-leadership skills—if they don't come to the office with the right emotional state and an optimistic attitude—then nothing I do with the entire leadership team will have much impact.

Here are some symptoms that will help you understand where you have opportunities to work on your self-leadership.

YOU COMPLAIN ABOUT STRESS AND TOO MUCH WORK

I worked with one CEO who always looked frazzled when she

came into our monthly leadership team meeting. She'd enter the room with a disorganized stack of reports and documents and immediately complain about how tired she was, how late she worked the night before, and how much more work she still had to do.

As I looked around the table, I could see the apprehension in her leadership team's faces. Seeing their boss so stressed and exhausted worried them and made them feel stressed as well. What's worse is that the CEO seemed to accept this harried state as the status quo. She didn't encourage a healthy conversation that would look at her problems and find solutions. It was as if the CEO wanted to continue feeling beleaguered for some reason—possibly to show how vital she was to the operation or maybe because she was trying to inspire others to work as hard as she did.

Whatever it was, it didn't work.

YOU BLAME OTHERS

We've all had bosses who think their greatest skill in life is determining who to blame when something goes wrong. These folks have what psychologists call an "external locus of control." In other words, if sales are off, it's the sales manager's fault. If inventory is down, it's the production manager's fault. If the leadership team is lethargic, isn't bringing good ideas to the table, and isn't holding each other accountable, then this CEO wonders why he shouldn't fire them all. These CEOs think the problem is external to them.

As long as a problem is external to you, it's almost impossible for you to fix it.

YOU ARE AFRAID TO LET GO

Many companies evolve from one person doing 95–100 percent of the work at their kitchen table. That person never takes vacations, and when they hire, they hire people as helpers or for administrative tasks. Everyone has specific roles, and the owner's job is to tell everyone what to do.

However, at some point, the business grows, and the owner needs to build a leadership team. When that need arises, many owners struggle to transition from being the person who has all the answers to being someone who relies on others to make smart decisions. The leaders think they have to have all the answers and control, and as a result, they don't let others on the leadership team find answers or be accountable.

The problem with this is that the company will never get better than the leader. Remember the law of the lid? CEOs who insist on continuing to be the smartest person at the table can actually hold their company back. If all the key decisions have to go through or emanate from the CEO, it creates a bottleneck that can restrict growth. Furthermore, others on the leadership team might be better equipped than the CEO to find the right answer.

YOU'RE INCONSISTENT

Another sign that your emotional state is controlling your behavior is when you send mixed signals to your direct reports. One day, you micromanage, and the next, you give people too much rope. Sometimes you're fun and laid back, and other times you're serious and tense. You don't own or control your emotional state.

The result is that employees and other members of the leadership team become tentative. They shift from solving problems to anticipating what you as the leader are going to ask for. They hold back, and as a result, productivity declines and stress levels climb.

SELF-LEADERSHIP: AN ACTION PLAN

Members of a Breakthrough Leadership Team understand the importance of self-leadership. They understand that they need to continually grow and learn, both in business and in their personal lives. They know their strengths and weaknesses, and they build a team around them that dovetails with those characteristics in a way that allows their company to grow. They start with an idea of what role they want or need to play in their organization, but the truly successful ones craft a role that leverages their personal strengths while compensating for any weaknesses.

Here are the critical self-leadership actions leaders need to take to create a foundation for building their Breakthrough Leadership Team.

MANAGE YOUR EMOTIONAL STATE

This is the first and foremost thing a leader has to keep in mind. If people in the company see that you have this grim expression all the time, they think, *If the boss is so worried, I should be worried!* By the same token, if you have an optimistic, high-energy attitude, that's contagious to the rest of your organization.

Stress is a natural part of life in business. An entrepreneur, business owner, or CEO wants to challenge themselves every day to do something more or different or better, and by doing that, we bring stress on ourselves. There's always that next dragon to slay because, otherwise, we'd get bored or get left behind by our competitors. In this sense, stress is not a bad thing. Stress drives you to learn and get better.

Just as you must manage your stress, it's also imperative that you find a recipe for cultivating your personal happiness. You need two strategies: one to prime yourself for the day ahead and one to manage unexpected events during the day.

Here's an example of how one of my clients primes himself each morning for the day ahead. First, he does fifteen minutes of meditation, followed by forty-five minutes of exercise. Then he spends ten minutes reflecting on specific things he's grateful for and fifteen minutes reading books that deliver positive, upbeat messages. All this puts him in an optimistic mindset that leads him to greater success. Many successful people have a routine like this for both the morning and evening. They commit to the process.

But what do you do when something happens during the day that throws you off your game? What do you do if you have a setback or an unfortunate encounter with someone, and you're struggling to keep that negative event from spiraling in your mind and distracting you for the rest of the day?

Below is a short list of some priming and midday actions that have worked for me:

- Meditation—Fifteen minutes of mindfulness in the morning and evening will give you a calm, focused, and more present mind. I use an app called Headspace, but there are many methods that will work.

- Gratefulness—Spend some time writing down the things you're thankful for. You can't be grateful and stressed or angry at the same time.

- Exercise—There are many studies detailing the positive

effects of exercise on the brain. When I exercise in the morning, I have more energy and clarity throughout the day.

- Listening to music—When I'm feeling stressed or down, all I need is a little AC/DC "Back in Black" or Led Zeppelin's "Kashmir," and I'm ready to take on the world.

- Taking a long walk—Sometimes, just separating myself from a stressful situation by taking a walk is enough to get my head back on straight.

- Affirmations—See more details in the section below.

USE AFFIRMATIONS

Affirmations are empowering, positive thoughts that, if you say them over and over again, actually rewire your brain. You need to make sure your beliefs are in line with what you want to achieve.

A few examples of good affirmations are:

- I have an extraordinary ability to accomplish everything I choose and want.

- I am a success in all that I do.

- I am a powerful and resourceful creator.

- I feel happy and at peace with myself.

- I live each day with passion and purpose.

Several years ago, I was asked to give a talk to a group of real estate agents in Paterson, New Jersey, about how to have a positive attitude. This was right after the real estate bust in 2008, so I had my work cut out for me. What's more, the owner of the real estate office called to let me know that some of the agents in his office were upset because he was making them stay late. *Oh, great*, I thought. This is starting to sound like a recipe for failure.

Then I hit traffic.

So now I was sitting in traffic, and I was going to be late to talk to a group of disgruntled real estate agents who don't really want to listen to me. I was ready to punch the steering wheel. But when the traffic had me totally stopped, I pulled out my phone and read through my affirmations. I repeated the affirmations out loud, and when I finally arrived (fifteen minutes late), I was walking on a cloud. Affirmations fill your brain with empowering beliefs, as opposed to the negative and stressful chatter that typically fills our heads.

CREATING A GREAT AFFIRMATION

Here are some of the qualities of a good affirmation:

- **It starts with "I am."** *Chicken Soup for the Soul* author Jack Canfield says these are the two most powerful words in the English language. He also advises that you keep your affirmations in the present tense.
- **It's brief and specific.** Canfield notes that some affirmations describe a goal in its already completed state. For example, say you are training to run the Boston Marathon. Your affirmation leading up to the race might be, "I am happy and grateful that I am now crossing the finish line of the Boston Marathon," and you would say it as you picture yourself running effortlessly through Copley Square.
- **It's positive.** It's crucial that your affirmation avoid words like "not" or "don't." Your subconscious does not process negatives. For example, if I told you not to think of a purple tree, what immediately comes to mind? A purple tree, of course. If your affirmation is "I am not broke anymore," your subconscious will focus on the being "broke."
- **It's repeated regularly.** If you say your affirmations at least three times a day, they become an automatic way of thinking.
- **It becomes a habit.** You must repeat your affirmations for at least twenty-one days straight if you want to change your habit. If you miss a day during that twenty-one-day period, start all over again until you have twenty-one days straight.

DEVELOP AN INTERNAL LOCUS OF CONTROL

An internal locus of control means that when you are confronted with a problem—regardless of the source—you take responsibility for addressing it. You don't blame others when things go off track. Instead, you ask, *What role did I play in letting this happen, and what can I do to fix it?*

Let's say, for example, that I'm a CEO who's very frustrated with his leadership team. They all leave exactly at five o'clock, even if the work isn't done, and they don't hold each other accountable or care about the purpose of the company.

If I had an external locus of control, I would point the finger at them and say, "This leadership team is letting me down! Why don't they do x, y, and z?" Those thoughts aren't going to do much good because as long as a problem is external to you, it's impossible for you to exert any real level of control to fix it.

An internal locus of control means I take responsibility for actions, even when the problem is not my fault. Instead of blaming my team, I acknowledge that *I hired them in the first place* and then take steps to correct the situation. I develop better ways to communicate our purpose and vision to instill more ownership in my team, or I start actively weeding out the toxic C-players. I make the problem my responsibility; only then can I take corrective action.

For people with an internal locus of control, problems are lessons.

These people focus on what they can learn and how they can act. To external-locus-of-control people, problems are an intrusion in their lives. When they experience a problem, they quickly determine how others need to change for the situation to improve.

Here are some examples of the shift between an external and internal locus of control:

EXTERNAL	INTERNAL
He just doesn't get it.	How can I do a better job communicating so he understands?
My team doesn't seem to care about our results.	How can I do a better job instilling a sense of ownership in my team?
Our clients are so unforgiving whenever we have a problem.	What can we do to create stronger, more loyal client relationships?

LOOK FOR THE POSITIVE

This is another simple trick that works. By focusing your brain on a particular outcome, you're more likely to experience that outcome.

If you attend a networking event and think, *I hate these things; they never amount to anything,* that's probably the result you will get. If your first conversation is with someone who says, "Oh, you're the CEO of a marketing firm? I just hired a new marketing firm," you're likely to see that as confirmation of your thoughts. *This person is not even a prospect for me,* you think to yourself. *I knew this event was going to be a waste of time.*

On the other hand, if you approach the event thinking it will offer you opportunities, that conversation might have a different result. Instead of being discouraged because this person already has a marketing firm, you might think, *Wow! How cool is this? The first person I talk to is someone who believes in what I do! Perhaps this person can introduce me to some friends who are also looking for marketing help.*

START WITH THE GOOD NEWS

I start all of my client meetings by going around the table as everyone on the leadership team shares a win or a piece of good news (personal and professional).

Some team members don't embrace this approach at first. They think the good news exercise is a waste of time. They're more eager to shorten any time sitting in meetings so they can have more time to focus on resolving the problems waiting for them. It's not surprising that they feel this way. Business leaders are always striving to reach a higher place, and to do that, you have to overcome all kinds of barriers. Even if they've had a recent victory, they are still more likely to look ahead to the next obstacle.

But it's also a recipe for burnout. If your leadership team is only talking about the negative issues, they tend to forget all the good things happening. They start to think, *Damn, we have a lot of problems! Why the hell are we doing this? Is all this effort really worth it?*

Focusing—at least for a time—on the good news helps you see more good news. And when you see more good news, you start to see more opportunities. A good example is when you buy a new car. Suddenly, you start to notice a lot of people are driving the same make, model, and color. It's not that suddenly everyone copied you and bought that car. It's just that whatever you focus on, you see more of. The same thing happens when you get your leadership team focused on their successes before they tackle their obstacles.

TRY JOURNALING

One way for CEOs and other business leaders to avoid obsessing over missteps is to keep a journal and record all of your wins, both large and small. I add to mine throughout the day because I want to stay focused on these wins rather than on the one thing out of ninety-nine that went wrong. If I'm not focused on successes, I'll obsess about that one mistake.

If you always look for good news, you'll find more good news to bolster your confidence—a key ingredient of business success.

ADOPT A GROWTH MINDSET

In her book *Mindset*, Carol Dweck talks about a growth mindset versus a fixed mindset. A fixed mindset is when you believe your skills and the skills of the team around you are static: people are either talented or they aren't, or they're either going to do a great job or they won't. A fixed mindset doesn't take into account the power of hard work. Dweck points out how some parents err when they tell their kid, "Great job getting an A on that test! You're so smart!" Instead, they should be saying, "Wow! Congratulations on earning an A on that test! You really worked hard to prepare for it!"

A growth mindset is when you believe you and everyone on your team can grow and get better and continuously improve. With a growth mindset, you challenge yourself and others around you to get better. A growth mindset drives a beneficial obsession with personal development. It drives you to want to be coached and to want to be a great coach for others.

TRUST AND LET GO

We've already talked about leaders who want to be involved in every decision, either because they don't trust their employees or because they think, as the leader, they have to have all the answers. When the company is faced with a problem, this CEO pulls the leadership team together and says, "Okay, here's what we're going to do: Joe, you do A, B, and C, and, Sally, you take care of D, E, and F. Go make that happen and come back and tell me what you did."

But as soon as Joe hits an obstacle, he's back in your office, wondering what he's supposed to do. Sally's out in the hall, waiting to ask you something else. You've tried to be an assertive leader, but in the process, you've undercut your leaders and reduced them to the role of helpers.

But what if you approached the problem a different way? You may already have a great solution in mind, but instead of barking out orders, you ask your team, "Okay, guys, we've got this problem. What should we do?" The team discusses the issue. One of two things are going to happen, and both are powerful:

1. The team determines an approach that is better than what you had in mind.

2. The team argues and debates the issue and ultimately reaches the same conclusion you did.

In both those scenarios, you come out ahead because now *your team* owns the solution. It's not just you. They have a personal stake in the outcome. Now when Joe hits that obstacle, he's not going to look back to you and say, "Okay, genius, what do I do now?" Joe helped formulate the solution, so he's going to climb over the wall, go around the wall, dig a tunnel under the wall, or just knock the damn thing down. Joe is going to be driven to succeed, whereas in the original scenario, his role was merely to carry out your orders.

It's crucial that as a business leader, you learn to trust and let go. Let your team have some impact. If you don't, you're not going to keep great people, you're not going to scale your company, and you are going to be frustrated because you have to approve everything. You have to do all of the hard thinking because you've trained your good people to stop thinking and to just take orders from you.

ASK MORE THAN TELL

A lot of the CEOs I work with have to learn when to remain silent and let the rest of the leadership team talk. For example, when I meet with a team and raise a question about the company's strategy, the CEO often jumps in with a quick answer. Everyone else at the table regards the CEO respectfully and nods in agreement.

They may truly agree with the leader's answer. But if they disagree, we'll never know what their answer was because they don't want to contradict the CEO. Again, the leader is slamming a lid down on the company by not letting the rest of the leadership team talk.

A great leader needs to be a great coach, and a great coach doesn't give the answers. A great coach asks the right questions and gets everyone else thinking.

LEARN CONTINUOUSLY AND IMPROVE

Just as the entire leadership team must be constantly working to improve, the leader has to regularly focus on their own development. They should be avid readers, attend seminars, and hire a coach. They should formulate a plan for their personal growth.

As in nature, if you're not growing, you're dying. You need a list of books to read, podcasts to listen to, and conferences to attend. You also need to hire people who will challenge you to be better and to learn more.

You'll find much more about personal and professional development in Chapter 6, "Developing and Improving Your Team."

FIND AND LEVERAGE YOUR NATURAL TALENTS

As I mentioned earlier, we all have natural talents and strengths. For example, some CEOs are outstanding salespeople. They may be horrible at the administrative part of their job, but they have a natural gift for convincing people to buy their product.

One of the great things about being the leader is that you get to craft your role. If you're smart and proactive about hiring the right people, you can design your role so that you spend 80 percent of your time working on the things you love to do and leverage your unique talent. As Marcus Buckingham and Ashley Goodall detail in their book *Nine Lies about Work*, we have the most potential for growth in our areas of strength, not weakness. When we add knowledge, skill, and passion to our natural talents, we get superstar performance and a love for what we do. Trying to strengthen a weakness is an uphill battle that saps our energy and passion.

Most people aren't aware of their natural talents because when something comes easy to you, you think it's something anyone can do. For example, when I owned a staffing and recruiting business, I hired a staffing supervisor named Kim who had a knack for quickly assessing people. She could tell in just a few minutes whether a candidate she was interviewing was trustworthy and a good match for the opening we were trying to fill.

I didn't have the same skill. I would form an immediate impression of someone and then spend the next twenty-five minutes of the interview justifying my first impressions and not gleaning any new information from the candidate. As a result, many of the people I sent out on jobs turned out to be unreliable and unskilled.

When I told Kim how impressed I was at her innate ability to assess people, she looked at me like I was nuts. "Anybody can do that," she said.

"No, Kim, not everyone can do what you do. Look at all the mistakes I've made in hiring!"

When you have an innate ability, it's hard to imagine that others might struggle with that skill. As we get older and deeper into our careers, many of us become more aware of our strengths, but it always helps to take an assessment or have someone hold up a mirror for you.

Once you've identified your natural talents (see the callout

"Finding Your Natural Talents"), ask yourself the following questions for each talent:

1. What will you do to turn this talent into a strength (or greater strength)? How will you increase knowledge, skills, and practice?

2. How will you better leverage this talent/strength every day? How will you commit to giving these gifts to the world?

In Chapter 6 ("Developing and Improving Your Team"), we will describe an exercise you can use as a leadership team to understand the natural talents on the team and coach each team member to leverage those talents.

FINDING YOUR NATURAL TALENTS

There are a number of ways to determine your natural talents:

• The Clifton StrengthsFinder (www.gallupstrengthscenter.com/home/ en-us/strengthsfinder) is an online assessment that reveals what you do best naturally and how to develop your talents. The assessment (and accompanying book *StrengthsFinder 2.0* by Tom Rath) helps you explain to others what your natural abilities are.

• The University of Pennsylvania's Authentic Happiness website (www. authentichappiness.sas.upenn.edu/home) has the VIA Character Strengths Survey (www.viacharacter.org/survey/account/register). It is a free, fifteen-minute character test that reveals your greatest strengths. You can also get a detailed report for a fee.

DISCOVER YOUR BLIND SPOTS

At the other end of the strengths spectrum are your blind spots or potential weaknesses. These are areas where you have no natural talent or passion.

For example, I tend to be good at spotting simple answers to complicated problems. However, early in my career, I wasn't very skilled at seeing how others might be affected by my actions or my words. I lacked empathy.

I remember sitting in a meeting, and a colleague was at the whiteboard sketching the diagram of a problem we were facing. It was a difficult problem, and the whiteboard was a mess. My colleague was struggling to find a solution. But I could see the answer clearly, so I jumped up, grabbed the marker from him, and said, "All we need to do is A, B, and C." I sketched it out, and it made sense to everyone.

I thought I was a hero, and it wasn't until later, when I ran the meeting through my mind again, that I realized I had stepped on this poor guy and had probably made him feel incompetent. I'd solved the problem, but at what cost to my relationship with him or to my reputation? I've gotten better over the years, but I always have to be aware that I have this blind spot.

The problem with blind spots is, of course, we're blind to them. If we can't see them, how do we know they're blind spots? I've found two helpful ways to reveal your blind spots:

1. **Take a DiSC Assessment.** This assessment will help you to understand your natural tendencies as well as your potential blind spots. It focuses on how you think and communicate. There are many versions of DiSC, but I like the one from Wiley at www.everythingdisc.com.

2. **Ask for feedback.** Ask each member of your team the following question: "What do I do that detracts from our team?" When you get the answer, either ask for clarity if you don't understand their response or say, "Thank you." Take their feedback with gratitude. Don't disagree even if you do. Getting into an argument with them about their feedback is a sure way to never get honest feedback again.

Once you find a weakness or blind spot, what do you do? Your immediate reaction might be to try to fix the problem by improving in that area.

Very often, that's the wrong answer. You might improve enough to become mediocre in an area of weakness, but you'll never be great. And, as I said in the last section, you'll sap yourself of energy and passion in the process.

When you identify a weakness, delegate that type of work to

someone who enjoys doing it and excels at it. Your weakness is someone else's strength, and if your leadership team has been structured properly (see Chapter 2, "Structuring Your Leadership Team"), team members should complement each other. Chances are someone on your team hates doing what you love and vice versa. Figure these out and leverage each person's innate abilities.

Your job as a leader is to surround yourself with people who are strong where you're weak, who see clearly where you're blind. Don't fix your weakness. Make it nonexistent by not having to perform in that area.

Still, some weaknesses you're just going to have to overcome. For example, I'm working with a member of a leadership team who gets flustered when he's put on the spot with a question. He wilts when another member of the leadership team asks him a question. His confidence evaporates, and he can't add two plus two.

That's a weakness he can't delegate. He's just going to have to get better about communicating and thinking on his feet. He may never be an expert at this, but he knows he's got to get better.

Instead, focus your efforts on your strengths. You won't create a great company through a group of leaders focused on improving weaknesses and becoming mediocre at best. You *will* create a great company through a group of leaders who are focused on their strengths and passions, and are doing great work.

THAT NIGHT WITH RICHIE

When I think back to the story I shared at the top of this chapter—of coming home in a bad mood and triggering the week from hell by yelling at my son—I realize how much I contributed to my own problem. In the heat of the moment, I did not adopt an internal locus of control. I did not take responsibility. Richie didn't behave any differently that night than he had on previous nights, yet the result was much different because of the way I behaved.

In any situation, there is a moment when we can regain control. There is a moment when, even if I feel like I'm totally justified in screaming, that I can stop and reconsider. On that night with Richie, I needed to take advantage of that moment and perhaps even stretch it out for some time by walking away or going into another room and cranking up "Kashmir" by Led Zeppelin.

We can all change how we behave, and we need to be aware of that. Because if you change yourself, the world around you will change as well.

This is what leaders need to remember. It's easy to blame everyone else, so when I hear a leader ranting and raving about their terrible leadership team, I have to ask, "Who hired them? Who's leading them? Who's coaching them?"

You. So if you have a poorly performing team, look in the mirror. You created this. But you can fix it too.

CHAPTER 2

STRUCTURING YOUR LEADERSHIP TEAM

I worked for a time with a family-owned company that made and distributed consumer products. They were big in the Southeast and Texas. But the company was growing at a rate of only 3 percent a year, so one of the family members—the cousin of the CEO—asked if I'd help reshape the company's leadership team.

Although the company had a somewhat traditional leadership team structure, three of the company's most important functions—marketing, sales, and production—were all under one person, a smart, hardworking guy named Steve. To me, one of the answers to the company's weak-growth problem was simple: take two functions off Steve's plate and let him concentrate on his area of expertise—production—and find some A-players to run sales and marketing. With more bandwidth for production, sales, and marketing, they had a chance to increase that growth significantly and expand to other markets.

Since Steve had been with the company for twenty years and wasn't very receptive to the change (it would shrink his little kingdom), the CEO was unwilling to make the change. In fact, he wasn't very receptive to looking at any structural changes on the team. That was the first example of many that showed he wasn't very coachable. There wasn't much point in my sticking around if the CEO wasn't going to do anything differently, so I parted ways with them.

I tell this story because it illustrates one of the more common reasons companies struggle to grow: they fail to take a methodical approach to structuring their leadership team. They don't plan for their own growth, they overlook when their leaders are stretched too thin, and they miss opportunities to expand. In many companies like these, A-players are fleeing because of a lack of accountability and because the leadership is always scrambling from one emergency to the next. The A-players who stay are forced to become B-players because their workload is too heavy. Meanwhile, CEOs make snap, emotional decisions about hiring to quickly fill the void and relieve the overworked rather than carefully planning how to structure their leadership team.

It doesn't have to be that way.

SYMPTOMS OF THE PROBLEM

It's not hard to spot a company struggling with a poorly designed leadership team. Here are some of the signs.

POOR ACCOUNTABILITY

CEO: "Our inventory turn is much too high."

Me: "Who's accountable for inventory performance?"

CEO: With a confused look, "Well, our inventory plan is created by our production team. So I guess it could be a production problem. On the other hand, production can't help it if sales doesn't sell it, so it could be a sales problem. And of course, product development created the product, so it could be their fault too."

Poorly structured leadership teams typically have account-ability problems similar to the example above. It's hard to fix problems or leverage opportunities when it's not clear who the owner is. On poorly structured leadership teams, confusion reigns.

PEOPLE ARE STRETCHED TOO THIN

Leadership team members who are chronically stretched too thin are also a ticking time bomb. They've been A-players their entire career, but they start to perform like B-players as their performance and attitude suffers. This has a cascading effect on their direct reports as well as the rest of the leadership team.

In smaller, fast-growing companies, the CEO is often at the heart of this problem. They might be serving as the head of the company, but they are also overseeing sales and traveling 75 percent of the time. Things start to slip through the cracks and hurt the rest of the company.

POOR HIRING DECISIONS

That kind of ragged emotional state can lead to some bad decisions, such as when the frustrated and overworked leader says, "That's it—we need to hire a head of sales," places an ad on Craigslist, and hires the first candidate through the door. Was that candidate the most strategic hire? Probably not.

As we'll see in the next chapter, even proactive companies make hiring mistakes. Even when their goal is to hire all A-players, most companies succeed merely 25 percent of the time. But, as we'll see in Chapter 3, there are ways to increase that success rate significantly.

LACK OF CLARITY

Most organization charts are pretty simple: the CEO is at the top and the leadership team falls in below.

But what if the CEO is also heading up research and development? The traditional org chart wouldn't list the CEO twice, so the fact that the company even *has* an R & D department isn't clear from the company's own org chart. In the case of the consumer products company I worked with, how were we supposed to depict Steve's responsibilities? Put his name down three times under the CEO?

What happens in these situations is that the leadership team has to play whack-a-mole as a series of problems pop up—insufficient inventory, new trucking regulations, or declining leads—and the company doesn't have someone to take responsibility for them. As soon as the company fixes one problem, another one pops up. And by the time the team finally adds someone to their leadership team, they've already lost clients and blown some opportunities to expand.

Fortunately, there's a better way.

STRUCTURING YOUR LEADERSHIP TEAM: AN ACTION PLAN

Structuring the right leadership team for your company requires that you anticipate problems and opportunities before they arrive. By being proactive, you can draw a blueprint for the leadership team you need now, as well as what that team should look like in the future. How does your leadership team need to change as your company's revenue grows, its product line expands, or its number of locations increases?

Breakthrough Leadership Teams plan changes to their leadership structure by carefully planning their growth over three years in quarterly segments. They may start the growth stretch with some people overseeing more than one function, but they are careful to gauge when growth will require the addition of a new leader to take over a function from someone else on the team.

In a $5 million company that is producing widgets, you might be the CEO as well as the head of sales. You produce 100,000 widgets, and you've got 100 clients. Over the next two years, you plan to grow to $10 million, producing 200,000 widgets for 250 clients.

At what point along your timeline will you need to turn over the sales function to a full-time head of sales? It's impossible to predict without projecting key financial metrics, such as revenue, profit, and cash. You also need to project nonfinancial metrics, such as the numbers of widgets, customers, orders, and full-time employees.

With these projections in place, you can make a much more "scientific" decision as to when a new head of sales is required. As the CEO, you calculate that you can handle up to four salespeople (in addition to all of your other direct reports). Therefore, if the projected number of salespeople increased from four to six in the fourth quarter of the plan, it makes sense to start searching for your head of sales sometime in the second quarter with the anticipation of hiring and onboarding someone before the fourth quarter.

You are planning ahead rather than waiting until the need becomes urgent. Urgent hiring needs at a leadership team level most often lead to poor hiring decisions, and critical tasks slip through the cracks.

That's a simple example that applies to just one function of your leadership team. To accomplish this proactive approach on a broader scale for a growing company, it's essential for you and your leadership team to follow a series of key steps, including:

1. Develop a functional accountability chart.

2. Draw your current functional organization chart.

3. Scale the organization using your twelve-quarter forecast and functional organization chart.

4. Prepare job scorecards for all company functions.

5. Identify your external team. (Note: this can be done at any step in the process.)

Since these steps work best when performed in the right order, let's go into more detail for each one.

STEP 1: DEVELOP A FUNCTIONAL ACCOUNTABILITY CHART

The first step in the process is for you to work with your leadership team to identify the eight to twelve major functions in your company.

List Your Core Functions

When I'm working with a leadership team on this, I have each person write down what they believe each key function is on separate Post-it Notes, and then I stick them on a flip chart and group like items together.

Fig. 2

Functions/Business Units	Accountability	Success KPI 1	Success KPI 2
HEAD OF COMPANY			
SALES			
MARKETING			
FINANCE			
HUMAN RESOURCES			
OPERATIONS			
INFORMATION TECHNOLOGY			
CUSTOMER SERVICE			
R&D			

I use a Functional Accountability Chart during this exercise. Figure 2 is a template. The first column of functions is prefilled in this example with nine of the most common functions. Use these as a starting point and add, subtract, or change these for your company.

Determine Who's Accountable

In the second column, you list the individual who is accountable for that function. It is important to note here the difference between accountability and responsibility:

- Accountability—This is the person who owns the function. It is their job to strategize, plan, and manage the performance of this function. One and only one person is accountable. Having more than one person accountable for a function means *no one* is accountable for that function.

- Responsibility—These are the people whose job it is to roll their sleeves up and get the work done. This could be one person or one thousand. The person accountable may also be responsible for the function, but not necessarily.

From this chart, you will often see one or all of the following three potential issues:

1. **More than one person accountable for a function.** For example, you may have three regional heads of sales reporting to the CEO. If three people are accountable, no one is accountable.

2. **No one accountable for a function.** For example, everyone in the company may have a responsibility to provide outstanding customer service, but you may not have identified the one person who owns the customer service function.

3. **One or more leaders stretched too thin.** A leader may be stretched too thin if they're accountable for too many functions. They also may be stretched too thin if you've defined a function as one thing (administration) when it's really three things: (finance, human resources, and facilities). Lastly, they may be stretched too thin when their skills have not scaled to handle the role successfully.

If you do this exercise and find the CEO is sitting in five different accountability seats, the leadership team might decide that is a problem that has to be solved immediately. Or it could decide to hold off addressing the issue right away. It might be okay to make the CEO accountable for R & D at the moment because the company doesn't have much research and development happening at this stage. But in two years, when the company plans to expand its product line, the leadership team will have to take another look at that issue and decide if the CEO is still the best choice for that seat. You must prioritize what needs to be solved now versus later.

How Is Success Measured?

The third and fourth columns of the Functional Accountability Chart tell us what key performance indicators we will use to measure the success of each function.

These columns aren't as easy to fill out as you might think. Using marketing as an example, how do you know your marketing team is successful? They've created a nice website and launched a snazzy email campaign, but do those activities make them successful? Not necessarily. Figure 3 shows some examples of success measures to give you a bit of a head start in your thinking.

Fig. 3

Functions/Business Units	Success KPI 1	Success KPI 2
HEAD OF COMPANY	Net Income	Employee Net Promoter Score
SALES	Revenue	Number of New Clients
MARKETING	Marketing Qualified Leads	Cost per Lead
FINANCE	Net Cash Flow	Length of the Cash Conversion Cycle
HUMAN RESOURCES	Employee Retention	# A-Players Hired
OPERATIONS	Order Fill %	Lead Time
INFORMATION TECHNOLOGY	System Uptime	Average Response Time
CUSTOMER SERVICE	Client Retention	Client Net Promoter Score
R&D	Number of New Products Introduced	Number of New Products in the Pipeline

The key in all instances is that you are collecting hard data that you can compare to past performance and current targets.

More detail about key performance indicators and measuring what matters is in Chapter 5.

STEP 2: DRAW YOUR CURRENT FUNCTIONAL ORGANIZATION CHART

Once you've filled out your accountability chart, draw out a functional organization chart.

A traditional organization chart (we've all seen these) is based on titles (see Figure 4).

Fig. 4

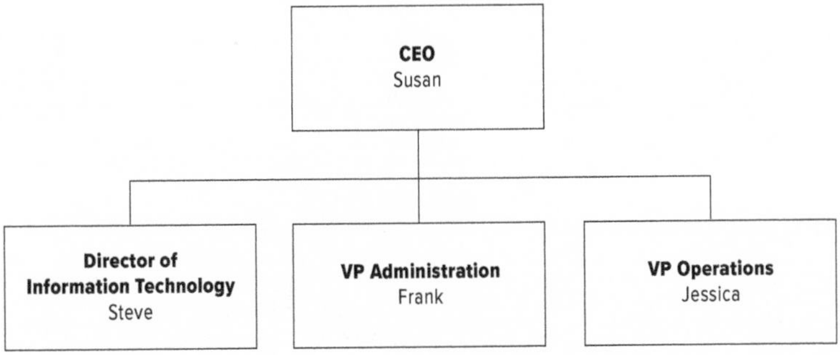

The problem with this type of organization chart is that it doesn't help you assess the current organization or plan for the future. Showing the CEO on the org chart without noting that she is also accountable for sales and marketing is misleading. Having a title like Vice President of Administration doesn't tell you anything about what that person is really accountable for. To create and scale your Breakthrough Leadership Team, you need something more descriptive and less static.

A functional organization chart is a more helpful tool than the traditional organization chart. A functional organization chart lists each function and the person who is accountable for that function (driven from the accountability chart we created). An *individual* in the traditional organization chart may have two or three areas of accountability, but you wouldn't know from looking at the diagram. However, in the functional organization chart, each *function* is listed, and the accountable person is named for each function. Figure 5 is an example.

Fig. 5

Head of Company — Susan					
Marketing Susan	**Sales** Susan	**Finance** Frank	**Human Resources** Frank	**Information Technology** Steve	**Operations** Jessica
1 Person	3 People	1 Person	1 Person	1 Person	3 People

The functional organization chart indicates that the head of the company, Susan, also oversees sales and marketing. Frank is the head of finance but is also accountable for human resources. You can also see the number of direct reports, which is one of the factors that help us decide if someone is being stretched too thin.

This picture of the current functional organization may not add much value on top of the functional accountability chart we've already created (it is simply a picture representation of the functional accountability chart). However, as we plan for future growth, this functional organization chart is invaluable.

STEP 3: SCALE THE ORGANIZATION USING YOUR TWELVE-QUARTER FORECAST AND FUNCTIONAL ORGANIZATION CHART

The next step in the process of proactively structuring your leadership team is to create your twelve-quarter forecast. As you forecast your company's growth each quarter, you'll modify the functional organization chart to ensure your leadership team scales to best support your growing company. Here's the process:

1. **Decide what numbers will drive the structure and size of your organization.** I would always start with revenue, net profit, and cash in the bank. You'll need some non-financial numbers here as well. Number of orders, clients, products, and units shipped might be good examples for a

product company. Number of clients, projects, and average size per project are some good examples for a service company.

2. **Forecast each of these numbers out three years, quarter by quarter, based on your desired levels of top- and bottom-line growth.** Forecasting out three years may not be easy, but it is necessary if you want to proactively support that growth. The leadership team must participate in this forecast. It should not be created by the CEO or CFO and just handed down to everyone else. Your entire leadership team should buy in and support this plan. See Figure 6 for an example.

Fig. 6

	2020 Q1	2020 Q2	2020 Q3	2020 Q4	2021 Q1	2021 Q2	2021 Q3	2021 Q4	2022 Q1	2022 Q2	2022 Q3	2022 Q4
Revenue	2.3m	2.4m	2.6m	2.6m	3m	3.2m	3.5m	3.6m	4.5m	4.7m	4.9m	5m
Net Profit	3%	3%	5%	3%	6%	7%	9%	8%	12%	14%	15%	15%
Cash in Bank	$100k	$150k	$160k	$175k	$200k	$300k	$500k	$750k	$1m	$1.4m	$1.7m	$2m
# Clients	85	95	105	115	125	137	155	175	200	220	240	260
# Orders	225	285	315	345	375	411	465	525	600	660	720	780
# Units Shipped	38,250	42,750	47,250	51,750	56,250	61,650	69,750	78,750	90,000	99,000	108,000	117,000
# Products	250	275	300	325	350	375	400	425	450	475	500	525
# FTE's	40	43	46	49	52	53	55	57	59	61	63	65

3. **Starting with the next quarter, create a functional organization chart for each subsequent quarter** by deciding what changes will be necessary given the forecast for that quarter. It will also be helpful to estimate the number of people needed within each function. The accompanying charts are examples based on the sample "Twelve-Quarter Forecast." It starts with the current state in Figure 7.

Fig. 7

Q2 2020

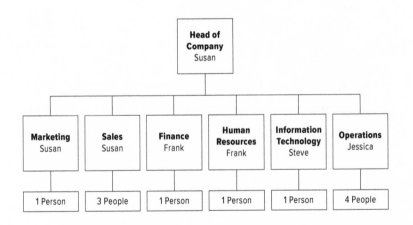

A. In Q3 of 2020 (Figure 8), an additional leadership team member (Sales TBD1) is forecasted to support both the sales and marketing functions as the size of the organization will probably stretch the CEO (Susan) too thin. Notice that the Information Technology team is also projected to increase, but with no impact to the roles on the leadership team.

Fig. 8

Q3 2020

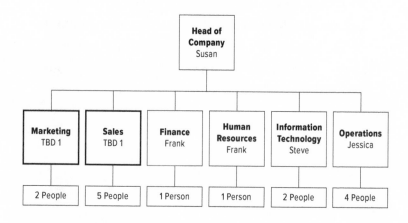

B. In Q2 of 2021 (Figure 9), as the sales team grows, adding a head of sales beneath (Sales: TBD2) the head of sales and marketing is forecasted due to continuing planned growth in the sales team. Notice the Finance, Human Resources, and Operations teams are also projected to increase, but with no impact to the roles on the leadership team.

Fig. 9

Q2 2021

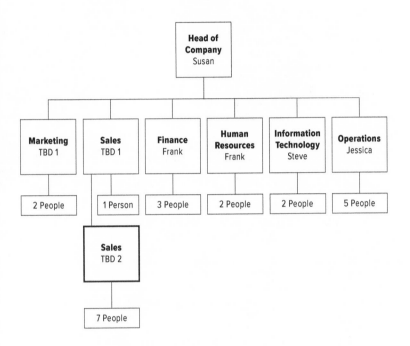

c. In Q3 of 2021 (Figure 10), a new head of HR is forecasted (Human Resources: TBD 3) given the number of company full-time equivalents (FTEs). Also, given the size of the operations team, a split of the organization between service and distribution is forecasted, with Jessica still heading up operations and service but with a new head of distribution (Distribution: TBD 4) who will report to Jessica.

Fig. 10

Q3 2021

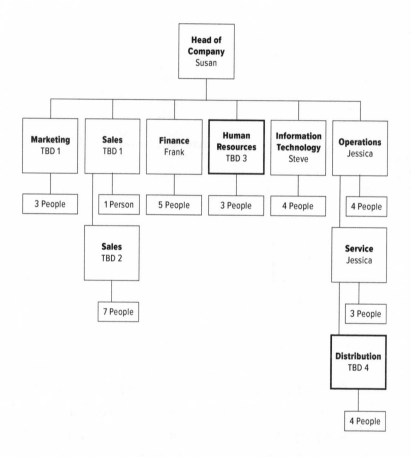

D. In Q1 of 2022 (Figure 11), it is forecasted that sales and marketing will split between two leaders (Sales: TBD 5), and a second sales leader (Sales: TBD 6) under the head of sales will be required.

Fig. 11

Q1 2022

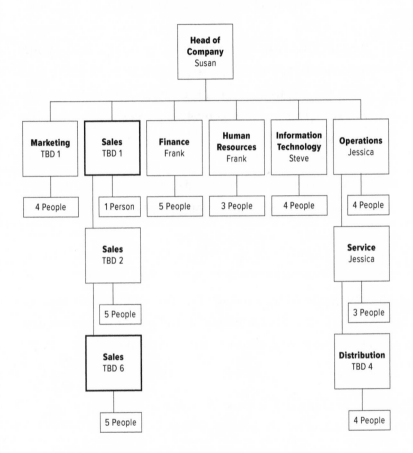

4. **Each quarter, at a minimum, the leadership team should use these forecasted functional organization charts to plan the actions necessary to update the structure of the leadership team.** These actions could include hiring someone from the outside (start this process at least two to

three quarters before you need to fill the role) or growing from within (start the professional development and coaching three to four quarters before you need to fill the role).

5. **Repeat this process each quarter by updating your forecast based on new information** and adding one more quarter to the end of the forecast. In this way, you will always have a rolling twelve-quarter forecast of your key numbers and results in a functional organization chart.

This process will seem difficult and inaccurate at first, but your accuracy will improve dramatically over time.

This twelve-quarter forecast is important for much more than just proactively planning the structure of your leadership team. Becoming proficient in this level of forecasting adds a level of sophistication to your strategizing and planning that will dramatically improve decision-making across the board.

STEP 4: PREPARE JOB SCORECARDS FOR ALL COMPANY FUNCTIONS

Once you have an understanding of your functional accountabilities and functional organization chart, it's time to develop more specific expectations for each leadership team function. You already have a head start on this from the success KPIs defined during the Functional Accountability Chart exercise. However, much more detail is required to ensure the function is understood in such a way that there can be no confusion as to how you're defining success.

When companies need to hire someone, most create a job description and post it to a hiring website or job board. The job description includes a brief explanation of the position, the type of tasks it performs, and the qualifications and experience potential candidates need to have. Applicants must have five years of industry experience, for example, or must know how to write programs in certain computer languages.

Frankly, this typical job description isn't that useful.

My favorite tool for this is the job scorecard developed by Bradford Smart in his book *Topgrading*. It's much more powerful and useful than the typical job description.

The job scorecard consists of:

1. The Job Mission—This is a short statement of why the job exists. For example, "The mission of the head of sales is to ensure we achieve our overall sales goals. He/she is responsible for hiring, managing, and coaching our sales force, tracking and optimizing our sales performance, and interacting with other areas of the organization to ensure top- and bottom-line growth."

2. Outcomes—Develop three to six specific, objective out-

comes that a person must accomplish to be an A-player. For example, "Grow sales by 25 percent in the next twelve months, build our West Coast sales team in the first six months, coach and recruit to achieve 90 percent A-players on the sales team within the next twelve months."

3. Key Competencies—Identify as many role-based competencies as you think appropriate to describe the behaviors someone must demonstrate to achieve the outcomes. For example, "Competencies include analytical skills, assertiveness, negotiating skills, coaching skills, and conflict management skills."

Next, identify five to eight competencies that describe your culture (these should include your core values, described in Chapter 4, "Defining the Right Culture") and place those on every scorecard.

Job scorecards should be created for all leadership team functions.

For new functions, the scorecard provides the foundation necessary to evaluate potential candidates (external or internal) to see if they're a fit for the position and to set expectations. Some leadership team candidates will take themselves out of the running for the position once they see the job scorecard and realize they're not a good fit.

For existing functions, the scorecard provides the foundation to ensure there is complete alignment on the expectations for the position. The scorecard should be used as the primary tool to periodically evaluate performance.

It's also important to discuss who should create all of these leadership team job scorecards. For an existing function, I've found that the best method is a collaborative effort between the CEO and the person accountable for that function. I recommend that the person accountable for the function create the first draft and review it with the CEO. This method results in greater functional ownership and less chance of the CEO playing too dictatorial a role. Once the person accountable for the function and the CEO agree on the details of the job scorecard, it should be reviewed by the rest of the leadership team. This is a critical step to ensure that there is leadership team alignment and a willingness to hold one another accountable for scorecards. For a new function, the CEO typically creates the first draft of the job scorecard. That draft is then reviewed with the leadership team and updated as necessary.

STEP 5: IDENTIFY YOUR EXTERNAL TEAM

To be a true Breakthrough Leadership Team, you'll need to do more than create a great internal team. These next three ideas focus on developing great external support as well.

Get a Coach

The right coach will provide a framework for growth, challenge you and the team to new heights, and help create an environment of discipline and accountability. A coach can guide and facilitate your leadership team strategy and planning sessions, as well as coach individual members of your leadership team. A coach will identify areas where you must improve and will hold you accountable. They can help you identify your blind spots and help you take steps to overcome them. What's more, a coach who also works with your leadership team gives the CEO an opportunity to *participate* in key discussions rather than merely facilitating them.

Join a Mastermind Group

A mastermind group is a small collection of like-minded individuals (external to your organization) who help you solve problems and challenge you to be your best. They could be other leaders in the same industry or different industries. Members use the experience and advice from other group members to solve problems, vet new ideas, or explore options for growth or change. A strong mastermind group will kick you in the butt when you need it, pat you on the back when you deserve it, and help unearth new ideas by sharing their experiences. Author Napoleon Hill introduced the concept in his 1925 book *The Law of Success,* described in greater detail with his 1937 book *Think and Grow Rich.* The idea has grown and has been refined over the years. A more recent book, *Who's Got Your Back?* by Keith

Ferrazzi, updates this approach and details how to create a mastermind group.

Two of the best-known groups for business owners and CEOs are the Entrepreneurs' Organization, or EO, and the Young Presidents' Organization, or YPO. These are not mastermind groups but have smaller mastermind groups within their membership (called forum groups). Forum members meet face-to-face once a month for daylong meetings to share ideas or common problems, and they participate in multiday retreats or trips. Forums are confidential, and members open up about personal issues as well as business concerns.

Some other examples of formal mastermind groups for CEOs and their leadership teams are Vistage (Vistage.com) and Cameron Herold's COO Alliance (COOAlliance.com). Many executives also form their own ad hoc mastermind groups, often using Ferrazzi's book as a guide.

I belong to two different mastermind groups. One group includes three other business coaches from around the country, and we meet on a video call once a month. Although we are all coaches, we specialize in different areas and typically have different goals for our companies. Despite these differences, we help each other by providing a sounding board. We celebrate each other's victories, providing our members a pat on the back when they need it or a kick in the butt if that's what will help them more.

I'm also a member of a second mastermind group called the CEO Roundtable. There are thirteen of us, and we're all business owners striving to grow and improve. Members come from a wide variety of industries—there's a head of an engineering staffing organization, for instance, as well as the head of a financial advisory firm and the owner of a marketing company. The group works because we all own businesses and can provide each other with different perspectives and experiences that other members don't have.

These groups are essential because leaders need people they can talk to and share their fears and successes with. Let's face it: it's lonely at the top. You can go home and complain about work to your spouse, but the best way to tackle your problems is to seek the help of someone who has faced similar problems and won. If I have a challenge, I can ask, "Have you grappled with this before? How did you handle it?" The input I receive is critical for success, so even though, as a leader, you are focused on building the right internal leadership team, don't overlook the value of an external team.

Hire a Professional Services A-Team

Your organization also needs an external team of professionals—an accountant, for instance, or a lawyer, banker, insurance agent, or business coach. I call this the Professional Services A-Team. The makeup of this A-team is almost as important as the makeup of your leadership team.

You absolutely need a strong accountant. I had one client who hired his accountant from Craigslist. Hmmm. Not the best hire. When I talked to the Craigslist accountant about how the accounts were structured and how he was categorizing expenses, I realized that I knew more about accounting than he did. If I know more than your accountant, you're in deep trouble.

I had another client who had been using the same outside accounting firm for several years. I referred the client to someone I trusted and worked with before, and in one meeting, this accountant had my client looking at his numbers in a new way that changed his business. Now my client is on his way to turning an unprofitable business into a strong moneymaker.

The right accountant is going to do more than fill out your tax return. The right accountant will work with you throughout the year to ensure you're analyzing your business and making more effective decisions.

Similarly, you need a great attorney to answer your questions about hiring, firing, contracts, trade secrets, or patent applications. You need a skilled and attentive banker who can help you with a line of credit, business loan, or other financing. You need an insurance agent who can tell you when you need more coverage or a different type of coverage.

These external services are vital to your business, and the best way to find them is by networking with people you know and trust and asking for recommendations. You don't find them on Craigslist.

CHAPTER 3

FINDING THE RIGHT PEOPLE

Kip Tindell made a name for himself when he opened The Container Store in Dallas in 1978. People loved the ingenious and attractive storage devices, from shoe racks and spice drawers to undersink organizers, and The Container Store soon expanded to nearly a hundred locations across the country.

But what really made The Container Store stand out was Tindell's attitude toward his employees. In 1999, The Container Store made *Fortune* magazine's list of "100 Best Companies to Work For"—a distinction it held for the next seventeen years.

Tindell's overriding philosophy about people was something he called 1 = 3. This is a belief that one great employee equals the productivity of three good employees.

I love this philosophy and have seen it at work. You can pay a superstar double what you pay a mediocre performer, and that superstar will still add more value per labor dollar than the mediocre performer. If you want a great company, you need a great team. Team members that are "good enough" won't get you there.

And when it comes to your leadership team, an A-player's impact is even greater. A-players in leadership can have more impact than five or even ten mediocre employees because of the number of people that your company leaders influence. They affect the rest of the leadership team, all employees reporting to them, clients, and vendors.

Your Breakthrough Leadership Team needs to consist of all A-players. As Jim Collins wrote in his book *Good to Great*, "Great vision without great people is irrelevant."

REDUCE THE GUESSWORK

You simply can't have B- or C-players on your leadership team if you hope to continue growing and building a company where people love to go to work every day. B- and C-players don't have the skills, drive, or strength of character to help your company succeed. A-players, on the other hand, are smart, savvy people who inspire others and often have skills and sensibilities that the CEO or other leadership team members lack.

This chapter defines a process that takes the guesswork out of finding the right people for your leadership team and increases your chances of having all A-players around the leadership table. This process won't eliminate hiring challenges and hiring mistakes. It will, however, raise your success rate from hiring 25 percent A-Players (the average hiring success rate according to *Topgrading* by Bradford Smart) to 75 percent or higher.

When you hire or promote the wrong person to the leadership team, that problem cascades down through your organization. If you have a fifty-person sales organization and you hire a mediocre vice president of sales, you now have a fifty-one person problem.

It's also a difficult mistake to rectify. Firing someone who isn't a good fit for your company affects your employees, disrupts your leadership team, and of course, has a major impact on the person you hired. There's an emotional impact, but there's also an economic impact. After adding up the cost of advertising, networking, interviewing, and onboarding, Bradford Smart estimates that hiring the wrong person costs a company fifteen times that person's annual salary. Factor in your company's lack of growth or other missteps brought about by the wrong hire, and your losses can go much higher.

A-PLAYERS HIRE A-PLAYERS

Taking your time to find and hire A-players for your leadership team is an investment in your company. That's because the people you hire for your leadership team are going to hire more people. Your CFO is going to hire accountants and analysts, and your head of sales will be hiring sales managers, salespeople, and sales analysts.

You want A-players making those hires because A-players hire other A-players. Superstars want to work with other superstars, so if you hire a superstar VP of sales, they're going to hire great salespeople. If you hire a B-player for VP of sales, they're very unlikely to hire A-players because:

- They don't recognize A-players.

- A-players want to work for other A-players. They see B-players as a poor reflection on the company and an obstacle in their way to growth.

- B-players are afraid of A-players because they see them as a threat to make them look bad or take their job.

In fact, while A-players hire other A-players, B-players tend to hire C-players. This is how a B-player on your leadership team can have a harmful effect on your workforce as these B-player leaders bring a parade of mediocre (or worse) workers into your company.

You can have a great strategy and a great new product, but if you don't have a leadership team of A-players, you will not become a great company. Your leadership team must be either all A-players or a combination of A-players and B-players who have short-term A-potential. You can't have C-players on your leadership team. B-players without A-potential will kill your business slowly; C-players will kill your business quickly.

OBSTACLES TO FINDING THE RIGHT LEADER

The obvious question then is, Why don't leaders hire only A-players for their leadership team?

As I mentioned earlier, finding the right leader is never an exact science. There are obstacles you'll have to navigate. Here are some of the more challenging ones:

THERE'S NO PROCESS

In many organizations, there is no defined process for sourcing, recruiting, and onboarding a new member of the leadership team. Each time there's a need to add a position or fill a vacancy, everyone scrambles. Do we have a job description? Where should we source our candidates from? Should we hire from within or go outside? Who should be involved in the interview process? How should we evaluate candidates?

The process (or lack thereof) is handled differently each time. There is no consistency, no real ability to learn from mistakes, and a low chance for success.

IT'S EASY TO GET FOOLED BY A NICE RÉSUMÉ OR BY A GOOD COMMUNICATOR

Anyone can create an impressive-looking résumé. It's easier to detect trumped-up résumés when hiring junior-level executives, but it's much harder to detect false claims at the senior level. Leadership team candidates have more experience and seasoning, and many are deft at exaggerating their skills and accomplishments in a way that seems reassuring. Many B-players skillfully portray themselves as more impressive than they actually are.

HIRING THE MOST TALENTED PERSON, NOT THE BEST FIT

There are many talented people out there. A much smaller percentage of those folks are a great cultural fit for your organization. Talent can be coached, but cultural fit cannot. For example, if a candidate for a leadership team position lacks a specific piece of industry or product expertise, that's coachable. But if they are a bad cultural fit (for example, they've got a hard edge, and your culture is one of respect and kindness), you've got a much bigger problem. Trying to coach someone to be a better cultural fit is like trying to get them to become someone they're not. They may be able to fake it for a while, but sooner or later, the original behavior will come back. And the company will suffer for it.

BOOTSTRAPPING THE LEADERSHIP TEAM

I have one client whose company is not as profitable as he'd like it to be. As a result, he's tried to find people for his leadership team who will accept less pay than the position is typically worth. He's found some seemingly "good enough" B-players, but now he's wondering why his company's growth continues to be stalled. He's the founder of the company and very talented, but he doesn't have anyone on his leadership team who is as intelligent, creative, or dedicated. None of them have the ability to challenge his ideas or challenge him to be better.

HIRING FOR THE PRESENT, NOT THE FUTURE

If you have a $10 million company, the tendency will be to hire someone for your leadership team who has the ability to be a strong leader in a $10 million company. That seems to make sense. However, if your plan is to be a $50 million company in the next five years, that leader may not have the ability to get you there. Most leaders hire to support their needs today without an understanding of how those hires will impact their plans for tomorrow.

NOT SEEING THE TRUE VALUE OF A-PLAYERS

I recently worked with a CEO who, in addition to heading up the company, was also involved in sales and HR. He worked in sales because he was good at it, but the only reason he worked on HR issues was because he'd hired a mediocre HR director.

The CEO had settled for a B-player because it would have taken longer and would have cost more to find an A-player.

The B-player was fine handling the tactical aspect of the job but wasn't particularly good at thinking strategically, creating the right culture, or developing talent. As a result, the CEO had to handle these functions even though he wasn't great at it and didn't enjoy it. With his time divided between sales and HR, the CEO wasn't effective in either role.

BELIEVING GREAT PEOPLE AREN'T OUT THERE

Because A-players are hard to find, many leaders start to believe they don't exist. The number of poor résumés, frustrating interviews, and hiring mistakes pile up in a leader's mind over time. The leader eventually decides the task is impossible and settles for a candidate who is "good enough." This launches a vicious cycle. If you believe it's impossible to find superstars, you stop investing serious time and effort in trying to find them. The more you shortcut the process, the less likely you are to find an A-player, confirming and solidifying the belief.

FINDING THE RIGHT PEOPLE: AN ACTION PLAN

A Breakthrough Leadership Team is made up of all A-players. If any B-players exist on the leadership team, they should have A potential within the next six months or they don't belong. Don't hire anyone onto your leadership team unless you believe they will perform as A-players quickly after onboarding. Each new leadership team member should raise the bar on your leadership team; average leadership team member performance should increase each time you add someone new to the team.

Finding A-players for your leadership team takes a tremendous amount of effort, as it should, since this is the most important job of the CEO and leadership team. An ongoing, rigorous process is necessary to both source, evaluate, and hire candidates. Here are some key parts of that process.

DEVELOP A VIRTUAL BENCH

The best way to find great people is not by running an ad and then reading résumés. That's probably the worst way to hire. Instead, the whole leadership team should be using its networks to identify and get to know great candidates, and this process should start long before you need someone.

If you have a growing company, you're always going to need good people. The best way to develop that pool of talent is through a process that *Topgrading* author Bradford Smart calls a "virtual bench."

Here's how it works: you make a list of ten leaders you know and trust from your industry or some other industry and you call them for an informal chat. "We're growing," you say, "and I'm wondering if you know any great A-players out there I should talk to."

"What position are you hiring for?" your friend asks.

"Nothing specific at this time," you say. "But I intend to grow significantly in the next two to five years, and to do that, I'll need great people, and I want to develop a list of A-players to keep on my radar."

With that, you start to get some names and you start contacting those people—not for a formal interview but in a friendly, get-to-know-you way. You might meet for coffee if they're in the same city or just talk on the phone if they aren't. "My friend Joe tells me you're a superstar. I don't have an opening right now, but we're probably going to have a need for people like you in the future, and I just wanted to get to know you."

So you chat. You tell them about your company and what your goals are. You find out a little bit about them. You ask the superstar about any of his friends who are also superstars. There is no pressure and no promises, but if the call goes well, you agree to stay in touch and to keep the lines of communication open.

You're building your virtual bench—for the leadership team as well as other key areas of your organization.

Building this virtual bench is a key part of every leader's job. If each leader just adds two to three people per month, you could have well over one hundred people on your bench in a year. And it's not enough to just start a list of names or to shoot off an email to a potential future hire. You have to develop a relationship with them. You have to talk to them, get to know them.

Now, if your head of sales is underperforming, you aren't as likely to keep them on and take on the task yourself while you desperately look for a replacement. You've got some names and phone numbers of great people. These A-players may have been happy with their jobs six months ago when you first called them, but now they might be looking to make a change. Perhaps you offer an intriguing challenge for them. I'm not saying someone from your virtual bench will be able to step in immediately—they still need to go through your hiring process—but if you do this right and talk with these folks on a regular basis, you'll have a sense whether they would be a good fit with your company.

The best way to build your virtual bench is by setting specific goals—contact a handful of people every month and have everyone on your leadership team do the same. All of a sudden, you have a pool of potential A-players, so when you need to hire someone, you've already established relationships with some great people. It's also important to keep your virtual bench "database" (it may be nothing more than a spreadsheet) in one central location to have a better handle on where your virtual bench is strong and where it's weak and requires more focus.

Mastermind groups (discussed in Chapter 2, "Structuring Your Leadership Team") are an excellent place to get names for your virtual bench. Another leader may have interviewed someone just last week who was outstanding but not right for the position. Or they may have a potential A-player internally who should be moved up, but there isn't an opportunity at that company to do so.

I DON'T HAVE TIME TO MAKE ALL THOSE CALLS!

When I talk to CEOs about building their virtual bench, many of them balk. In some cases, they don't want to ask anyone for help. More often, they claim they don't have the time. Unless they are hiring for a specific position, spending time talking to other leaders or potential hires doesn't seem like a high priority.

It should be.

As the CEO and as a member of a leadership team, there is nothing more important than surrounding yourself with the right people. No new strategy, product, or level of customer service is more important than finding A-players to work for your company—particularly if you're the CEO.

Your hiring process will be much more successful when you have a virtual bench. If you own a small company that grows to a point where you need a full-blown CFO instead of the current junior-level controller, wouldn't it be great to have five amazing CFOs on your virtual bench to talk to and invite to apply? Or would you rather post a job ad, hire a recruiter, and start poring over résumés from seventy-five strangers?

HIRE FROM WITHIN

Sometimes, the best candidate is someone already working for you. In fact, that's where you should look first.

If you're a $4 million business and you're just starting to put together a leadership team, it's unlikely you'll find a CFO among the current members of your team. It's just been you and a few folks you hired to crank out the product or the service, and it's unlikely someone with CFO experience or skills is in that group. But if you're a $100 million company, the chances that there is a potential CFO in your midst are much greater. This is particularly true if you've been scaling the right way and doing a good job with coaching, mentoring, and executing with discipline—things we'll discuss in Chapter 5.

The advantage of hiring from within is that you already know this person, they already know your company and its history, and they have been living your core values. Chances are they already understand the company's communication rhythms, procedures, and priorities. They already know the pattern of your company's planning and accountability. They're a known entity, and that's where you want to start when assembling your list of candidates.

One of the challenges of hiring from within your company is that the person promoted might not have executive credibility with the other members of your leadership team. That person may have been a sales manager before he became vice president of sales, but your leadership team still views them as a sales manager.

The best way to approach this is to give that person an opportunity while they are still the sales manager to drive high-profile projects that give them a chance to present, discuss, and debate with the leadership team. By the time they are ready to move up to the leadership team, the other members of the team are comfortable with them and understand their abilities. This also helps the sales manager feel confident that he or she belongs with the "higher-ups."

You know when someone is ready to be promoted when you see they are already acting in that capacity. For example, your sales manager proposes revamping your coaching program, and they come in to sell and debate that idea with your leadership team. If someone from outside the company were in that room and could easily mistake the sales manager for the vice president, then you know that person is ready.

HOW TO FIND THE HIGH-POTENTIAL LEADERS

With some of my clients, I facilitate an "accelerator session" each year that kicks off the annual planning process for the leadership team and helps spotlight the company's future leaders.

The accelerator session is a one-day meeting with the company's highest performers. Most or all of the participants report directly to someone on the leadership team. As the leadership team coach, I facilitate the sessions. The leadership team doesn't attend the sessions, but they join the group for the last ninety minutes to two hours as the results are presented. Depending on how big the company is, there could be ten to thirty people in the room. The session is held two or three weeks before the leaders' annual planning session.

We start off by breaking into smaller groups of four to six people, and each group does an analysis of the company's strengths, weaknesses, opportunities, and threats (SWOT). They put the results on flip charts and then discuss and debate their thoughts with the other groups.

Then we do a start/stop/keep exercise, in which each group lists three things the company should start doing in the next year, three things it should stop doing, and three things it must continue doing. These sheets go up and each group presents.

After that, each group examines ways their company can better embrace its core values. Maybe we need to change our interview questions because we're hiring too many people who don't have the values, maybe the company needs to do a better job of mentoring its employees, or maybe the company's not doing a great job of holding people accountable for living the values. Again, post on a flip chart and present.

Finally, each group zeroes in on what it thinks the company's top three priorities should be for the next year.

At this point, everyone takes a break, and I let the leadership team in. The leaders spend about fifteen minutes strolling around the room, taking notes about what they are reading on the flip charts and noting where they have questions. This is a treasure trove of information for them, and they understand that it's not acceptable to become defensive about what they're reading. (I coach the leaders on this before the session.)

Next, each group presents its findings to the leadership team and answers questions. Everyone gets an opportunity to present. The leaders can ask questions for clarification, but this session is not a forum to debate the ideas.

At this point, you can see clearly which employees are rising to the top. You can see who is leading and who is contributing and whose ideas are sticky and inspirational. Everyone is learning and getting to know each other, but some participants are really starting to stand out. Their words have real weight in the room.

The overarching goal is for the leadership team to get the unfiltered knowledge and ideas of their next-level leaders to use in their upcoming annual planning session. But an ancillary benefit is that the leadership team gets a sense of who the high-potential leaders are and who is standing out in the group.

PAY BIG BUCKS FOR EMPLOYEE REFERRALS

Don't forget that your employees are part of your network, so you should also have a strong employee referral program. Your employees—particularly your A-players—know your company and your culture, and they have a sense of who's going to be a good fit.

But you have to incentivize this. I see a lot of companies that have flimsy employee referral programs in which they pay the employee $500 if the person they recommend gets hired. You're not going to change anyone's behavior with a check that small. Meanwhile, you may pay a recruiter $60,000 to find a candidate for your leadership team.

Offer employees a greater incentive to be on the lookout for good hires. For example, you might offer employees something like $10,000 for a referral that gets hired. You pay $5,000 when the new employee comes on board and another $5,000 a year later—if the person they referred is still with the company. You don't want to pay so much that employees ignore their jobs and spend all their time recruiting, but you do want to offer enough to make them think, *You know what? Let me take some time this weekend and call some former colleagues to see who might be a good fit for this job.* Then, if their referral is hired, your employee also has an incentive to help that person succeed.

I've seen the following scenario play itself out dozens of times over the years.

- Month 1—The CEO begins to have concerns that the CFO she's hired is not performing at a level necessary to scale the company.

- Month 2 through 6—The CEO becomes more and more concerned as the CFO's projects are slipping and his team is becoming dysfunctional.

- Month 7—The CEO decides she needs to bring in a new CFO...at some point. Now is not the right time given how busy things are, so she puts it on the back burner.

- Month 8 through 11—The CFO's poor performance continues.

- Month 12—After more missed deadlines, the CEO decides she's finally had enough and fires the CFO. The CFO's work and all his direct reports now land on the CEO's desk.

- Month 13—The CEO, overwhelmed by the additional work, hires a new CFO after a one-month search in which she only interviewed three people.

- 3 Months Later—The CEO fears she might have made

another poor hire as the new CFO doesn't seem to be working out as she hoped.

Delaying the firing of an underperformer due to a fear of being short-staffed is called "the C-player trap." Leaders think, *If I lose this person now, I'll have a big mess to clean up.* So they wait until things "break" and they can no longer tolerate the person's performance.

So now it's been more than a year, and the poor performer has left all sorts of carnage in their wake—bad hires, poor results, dysfunctional teams. You've waited until the last minute to get rid of them, and now you are short-staffed and feel the need to hire someone quickly. Not only have you kept someone who was hurting your company, you're probably going to make the same mistake again because you're in a rush to hire a replacement.

What you've done is fire slow and hire fast, which is exactly the opposite of what you should be doing. If you're hiring too quickly, you're probably not evaluating the candidates as patiently and thoroughly as you should.

Research from *Topgrading* shows that the average cost of a mishire ranges from five to twenty-seven times the person's annual salary. A mishire for the leadership team will be even more costly when you factor in the lost productivity, onboarding costs, and low morale. And with the typical company hiring high performers 25 percent of the time (again, according to *Top-grading*), that means that 75 percent of the time, they actually incur those painful, costly mishires.

Finding A-players can take time. Most are not going to be immediately available because, as A-players, they already have jobs and are highly valued by their current employer. You'll need time and patience to convince an A-player to come work for you.

Firing fast and hiring slow is smart regardless of the position you're filling, but it's especially critical when you're hiring for your leadership team. A mediocre leadership team member is like a cancer in your organization. It's crucial that you cut it out as soon as possible because it is probably spreading to other areas of your organization. But it's also critical that you take your time to find and hire the right replacement. If you can replace that B- or C-player with a superstar, productivity is going to climb throughout your organization.

One important note: hiring slow does not mean moving slowly in interviewing and evaluating potential candidates. It means taking the time to find the right candidates. Once you find a strong potential A-player for your leadership team, your evaluation process (phone screen, interviews, etc.) should move swiftly. You don't want to miss out on a game-changing A-player because it took you three weeks to schedule a phone interview.

We talked earlier about how résumés can be deceptive. You may not be able to discern the truth in a résumé, but you can find truth from talking to the candidate about their résumé.

A *Topgrading* interview process decreases the chances that you'll mistake a B- or C-player for an A-player. I hope the *Topgrading* summary below convinces you to read *Topgrading* by Bradford Smart and/or the shorter companion book by his son Geoff Smart and Randy Street, titled *Who: The A Method for Hiring* to begin following the Smarts' process.

- **Job scorecard:** Start with a job scorecard as described in the previous chapter.

- **Work history screening.** Using a work history form, *Topgrading* companies dig into a candidate's past jobs, asking about salary history, manager assessments of the candidate's strengths and weaknesses, the most enjoyable and least enjoyable aspects of each previous job, and reasons for leaving past jobs. Every job they've had since graduating college is included, and the candidate is often asked about their expectations going into these past jobs, challenges they faced, responsibilities and accountabilities, significant accomplishments and mistakes, and the name and contact information for each person they reported to at the time. This detailed review exposes candidates who may have overstated their skills or accomplishments on their résumé, and since the same form is used for all candidates for a particular position, it saves you the time it takes to review individual résumés.

- **Phone interviews.** Candidates who meet minimum qualifications are screened in phone interviews that probe their professional goals, experience, and two most recent jobs. This is your opportunity to explain the job in more detail and to probe the candidate's responses on the work history form.

- **Competency interviews.** Different interviewers spend an hour with the candidate, asking questions about the competencies outlined in the job scorecard. This session gives candidates up to fifteen minutes to ask questions about the job, the organization's culture, strategy, and structure of the leadership team. A-players expect to be able to do this and appreciate the opportunity when they get it.

- *Topgrading* **interview.** This is a highly structured interview that can take one to three hours and includes questions about the candidate's education, previous work, goals, and personal assessment of their strengths and weaknesses. Interviewers ask up to sixteen questions about each of the candidate's full-time jobs from the beginning of their career to the most recent. Many companies use a tandem interview format in which two members of the leadership team conduct the interview (typically the CEO and one other member of the leadership team). When GE switched from one interviewer to two, its success rate for hiring A-players climbed from 50 percent to 80 percent. *Topgrading* interviewers gain deeper insights into a candidate, as they see the patterns of how they evolved in different past jobs.

- **Reference checks.** In the *Topgrading* system, candidates are responsible for setting up calls with their references, including bosses, peers, and subordinates. Candidates are reminded of this at every stage of the hiring process. This aspect of the process is what *Topgrading* calls the "threat of a reference check" or TORC and the "truth serum" because candidates are less likely to overstate their accomplishments when they know the interviewer is going to verify those claims with the candidate's former employer. Here's how it works: during the company's screening process, the interviewers ask candidates for the names of the individuals they reported to and how those individuals would rate them on a scale of one to five. Then they tell the candidate that before they can be hired, the candidate will be asked to set up reference calls with some of those former bosses. What's more, the candidate will request that the former boss be willing to have an honest discussion with them. This is when many of the B- and C-players flee, making every excuse possible. A-players, in contrast, are happy to call former bosses because they usually had a great relationship with them.

LOOK FOR CORE VALUES

Whatever process you use to evaluate leadership team candidates, one of your primary goals is to find out if this person is living your company's core values. We'll talk more about core values in Chapter 4 ("Defining the Right Culture"), but for now, I'll explain that core values in an organization are a set of nonnegotiable behaviors that anchor an organization's culture.

For example, in his book *The Ideal Team Player*, Patrick Lencioni talks about his company's (the Table Group) core values as "hungry, humble, and smart." By "hungry," they mean they are always looking for more: more things to do, more things to learn. By "humble," they don't mean thinking less of yourself. They mean thinking of yourself less and your team more. And by "smart," they mean people smart. Are you empathetic? Do you know how to communicate with different types of people? My company's core values are passion, learning, persistence, and focus on results. You have to find people who are already living your core values because it's unlikely they will suddenly become a different person after you hire them.

I have one client who has a core value that says, "We pick each other up." It's a culture of support, and the people who work there always look for opportunities to help their coworkers get better or enjoy more success. When the company's leaders are interviewing a candidate, they might ask, "Tell us about a time you were on a team and there was a team member who wasn't able to pull their weight." If the candidate responds by saying,

"I'd do their work for them if they can't keep up, but I'm not going to slow down for anyone when there's a job to do," this candidate may not be a good fit.

Business coach Shannon Susko is an entrepreneur who has launched and sold two startups and runs a consulting company called Metronome United. To find out if a candidate is a good fit, her company asks candidates up to ten questions for each of the company's core values. She has her entire leadership team involved in the interview process, and if one person on the team doesn't think a candidate fits the company's core values, the company doesn't hire the person.

That's how important core values are for successful companies. And whether a person embodies those values is not something you'll learn from a résumé. Again, these values are not negotiable or optional. Everyone must live these values. Someone may be incredibly productive, but if they don't live these values, they are toxic to the organization.

DON'T DRAG YOUR FEET

An ideal situation is when you have three great candidates for an open position and you have to choose one. However, that doesn't mean you should delay the hiring process if you only have one great candidate.

I had one client who had an excellent candidate for one of their leadership positions. Everyone liked this person, but the company took my advice to "fire fast and hire slow" to mean that they needed to find more candidates before making a decision.

That's not wise. When you have a great candidate, the last thing you should do is decelerate the process or drag your feet, hoping someone better will come along. That's how you lose A-players. Taking your time to find the right candidate does not mean moving slowly through the process. In fact, the opposite is true. Once you find an A-player candidate, you'll want to move through the process as quickly and efficiently as you can without skipping any steps.

REQUEST A PRESENTATION

Mark Nicholson, CEO of Zemax in Bellevue, Washington, one of the CEOs I interviewed for this book, understands the importance of hiring the right person. His company goes above and beyond the typical hiring process. Candidates for his leadership team don't just come in for an interview; they are asked to give a presentation to the entire leadership team, and several of the people who would report to that candidate are invited to attend.

Mark is purposely vague with the candidates about what their presentations should include. He may give the candidates a few topics he'd like them to cover—go through your experience and some of your achievements, for instance—but he wants the candidates to figure it out on their own. They are supposed to be leaders after all, right? Some candidates wing it and talk off the top of their heads, but others prepare formal presentations.

One thing Mark specifically asks candidates to include in their presentation is a thirty-, sixty-, and ninety-day action plan they will put in place if they get the job. What are you going to do when you hit the ground here?

This is something I haven't seen used with a lot of companies, but I think it's brilliant. The rubber meets the road right away, and people in the room can ask questions about the plan. A candidate who comes in with a detailed, well-researched plan makes a much different impression than someone who hasn't thought much about it and resorts to generalities.

The process is challenging for the candidates. It requires that they get to know the company ahead of time, and the best candidates will do some research into the personalities and core values of the company's leaders. The presentations often expose which candidates are B- and C-players (in fact, B- and C-players might just give up on the job at this point and not schedule the presentation), and give the leadership team and other employees a good look at how the candidate thinks and interacts with the people he or she will be working with. You can see how the candidate reacts when you challenge them, or how they incorporate new ideas from team members on the fly. Overall, this is a great way to "test drive" what it would be like to work with this person.

GET THEM OUT OF THE OFFICE

In his book *The Ideal Team Player,* Patrick Lencioni advocates getting candidates out of the formal interview setting. An interviewer can take the candidate to breakfast or invite him along while running errands, for instance. Organizational psychologist Adam Grant says that some CEOs will even call ahead to a restaurant and ask the staff to purposely mess up the person's order so the CEO can see how the person reacts and how they treat the wait staff. Grant believes the ultimate test of character is how you treat people who lack power.

I worked with one business owner who hired a new president. The first thing the new president did was take the leadership team out to dinner. It wasn't planned, but the restaurant messed up the president's order, and the leadership team sat in astonishment as the new president ranted and raved and belittled the waiter. It was no surprise that the president went on to be a dictatorial and demotivating leader. The leadership team had an inkling this would happen because of how he treated that waiter. They might have avoided a great deal of pain if the owner had learned this about the president before he hired him.

HAVE A SUCCESSION PLAN

Every member of the leadership team, including the CEO, needs to be on a constant search for successors within the company or from your virtual bench. There are two key reasons to be on a successor search.

First, you want to ensure that you have a strong talent pipeline to fill leadership positions if a new function is required (see Chapter 2, "Structuring Your Leadership Team") or if a leader exits the team and needs to be replaced.

The second reason is that as your company grows and complexity increases, the job of each leader will change. Members of the leadership team may need to refocus their efforts by widening or narrowing the functions they can and should spend time on. For example, the role of CFO at a $20 million company is very different from the role of a CFO at a $100 million company. When you identify a successor, it may not be someone who slides into your chair when you leave but someone who takes over the work you can no longer do as the CFO of a much larger company.

DEVELOP A PROCESS AND FOLLOW IT

Once you've implemented a process for the methods we've discussed in this chapter, it's crucial that you stick with that process for all candidates. Even when you have a superstar on your virtual bench who has expressed an interest in the opening you have, you must still follow the process. Do not deviate from your process, no matter how desperate you feel or how convinced you are that you have found a great candidate.

This is vital for a few reasons:

- **You may have a blind spot.** Your team members and key employees might see something about that person during the process that you hadn't noticed. They became key members of your company because they complement you, right? Take advantage of that.

- **You want your leaders and key employees to feel some ownership for the decision.** If they are involved and part of the decision to hire or promote someone, they'll have a stake in that person's success and will work to help them be successful.

- **The process exposes gaps in a candidate's knowledge or skillset.** Everyone will have gaps like this, but the process will help you determine if those weaknesses are coachable.

Finding the right people is not the last step to creating a Breakthrough Leadership Team. Even if you're successful in finding all A-players for your leadership team, it's vital that the team has the right culture. Read on to find out how that's accomplished.

CHAPTER 4

DEFINING THE RIGHT CULTURE

"Culture" is one of those words that is often misused, so let's start with a definition. I define culture as a set of beliefs and values that guide everyone in the company and are consistently followed. It becomes the personality of the organization.

A company's culture is critical to its success, and it starts with the leadership team. If you want a company with top-line growth, bottom-line profitability, and productive, enthusiastic employees who feel fulfilled with their work, you must have the right culture and employees who fit that culture. And you won't have that in your company if you don't have it on your leadership team. In fact, the interactions and symbiotic relationship of the leadership team members is more important than each of the leadership team members' individual skills.

Let's say your head of sales and head of service don't like each other and don't trust each other.

The head of sales says, "These damn guys in service are not getting my product out on time. They're constantly causing problems with my customers."

Then the head of service says, "These sales guys are promising things they should not be promising."

There is fighting back and forth and disrespect at the senior level.

When this happens, the discord is also going to appear at lower levels, and the problems typically get worse as they cascade down the organization. If you want a great culture at your company, it doesn't start with you asking, "How do we build culture for our company?" It begins with you asking, "How do we build the right culture in our leadership team? How should we be acting toward each other? What behaviors do we want to cascade down through the organization?"

During one of my work sessions with a leadership team, they began complaining about the morale in the company. "We do all these great things for our employees, but they're not happy," one leader said. "What's wrong with them?"

I had a suspicion of what the problem was, so I asked the leaders on the team to take a secret ballot. On a scale of one to ten, how likely are you to recommend working here to a friend or someone else you know?

Some of you will recognize this as a net promoter score, where your nines and tens are promoters (they will tell many people how great you are) and those scoring you zero to six are detractors (they will tell many more people how horrible you are). The sevens and eights are neutrals. You then subtract your percent of detractors from your percent of promoters to get your Net Promotor Score. When you do the math, you can get anywhere from +100 percent (excellent) to –100 percent (run!).

Their average rating was 10 percent.

That's not a number to be proud of, especially for a leadership team. That number would almost certainly be much worse if the rest of the organization were surveyed.

As we reviewed the results, I let the group know that it wasn't worth anyone's time to discuss employee morale. "You can't fix what's going on out there," I said, pointing at the offices outside the conference room, "until you fix what's going on *in here*."

WHY YOU SHOULD CARE ABOUT CULTURE

In 1992, two Harvard researchers examined two hundred US companies to determine whether a strong culture that valued employees and customers had any effect on the companies' long-term economic performance. Supermarket chains were compared to other supermarket chains, airlines were compared to airlines, etc. After analyzing these firms' financial performance over more than a decade, the researchers discovered that companies with "performance-enhancing" cultures—particularly those that focused maniacally on customers' needs and empowered all employees to lead the way in meeting those needs—simply killed the competition.

In net income growth, the twelve firms with strong corporate cultures enjoyed a 756 percent growth over eleven years, while twenty firms who were indifferent to culture grew at 1 percent.

In stock prices, those with culture saw 900 percent growth. Those without grew 74 percent.

In overall revenue growth, the culture-focused firms grew 682 percent while others grew 166 percent.

"Corporate culture can contribute meaningfully to financial results, and many people do not give this fact enough attention," said Dr. John Kotter, one of the researchers and the coauthor (with James Heskett) of *Corporate Culture and Performance*, later in a blog post for *Forbes*.

Fig. 12

	Average Increase for Twelve Firms *with* Performance-Enhancing Cultures	Average Increase for Twenty Firms *without* Performance-Enhancing Cultures
Revenue Growth	682%	166%
Employment Growth	282%	36%
Stock Price Growth	901%	74%
Net Income Growth	756%	1%

SYMPTOMS OF A WEAK CULTURE

Here are some of the signs that may help determine if you've got some work to do on your leadership team culture. Oh, and here's a little hint: you should *always* be working on your leadership team culture.

SILO FOCUS

Leadership team members are more concerned with their own team than they are with the success of the company. The head of sales is happy as long as sales are up, and the head of service is only interested in getting outstanding numbers for the service department. The overall effort is fractured at the top, and those cracks widen the farther down you go in a company. When you see unproductive conflict, silos, or selfishness at the lower levels of a company, that's almost always a sign that you have a culture problem at the leadership level.

IT'S NOT FUN

I knew ahead of time that my client's leadership team had problems even before they gave themselves a terrible net promoter score. Their meetings had no passion or energy. Their business was not growing, and people on the leadership team acted discouraged. Being around that team even sapped my energy. They were not having any fun.

MEETINGS ARE BORING

Breakthrough Leadership Team meetings are like a scene from a great drama. People are animated. They argue about ideas and then laugh about their differences as they stride off to accomplish the goals they all agreed to execute. Meetings with mediocre or weak teams, on the other hand, are dull and listless. People run through their statuses and then fall silent. They don't ask each other tough questions or vigorously challenge each other's assumptions. There's no drama, no energy, no action. If people are looking at their watches during the meeting and are anxious to leave so they can get "real" work done, you've got a problem.

ZOMBIE ISSUES

"Why are we discussing this again? I thought we resolved this last week."

"This is the third meeting in a row we talked about this, but we never make a decision."

This is a sign that your leadership team members aren't communicating enough, aren't communicating in the right way, or don't fully trust one another. Teams that aren't comfortable enough with each other don't tackle and resolve tough issues. The issues they do tackle are often left with no resolution or a fuzzy resolution at best. This results in something one of my clients calls "zombie issues"—issues you think are dead but keep coming back to life. The result is frustration and confusion.

THEY HAVE THE WRONG KIND OF CONFLICT

There are two types of conflict on a team—personality-based conflict and idea-based conflict. The first one is poison for your company, and the second one is a sign that your leadership team members trust each other—and that can be great for your team and your company.

About ten years ago, I worked for a short time with a client that had a particularly toxic culture on its leadership team. These people despised each other, and the CEO was clueless about it.

After our first meeting, he asked me, "What'd you think of the team?"

"I saw something today that I've never seen before," I said.

He gave me a quizzical look.

"We were here all day, and I did not hear one member of your team ask another member a single question."

"What? What do you mean? There were a ton of questions!" he said defensively.

"No," I said. "Those were condescending statements disguised as questions."

Here was a typical question I heard that day. "So, Bill, you really think by doing that, you're going to fix the problem?" That's not a question. That's someone saying, "Bill, you're a moron. That's not going to fix anything!"

When your leadership team is asking snide questions instead of earnest, probing questions, that's a sign you've got a culture problem. Breakthrough Leadership Teams with a healthy, positive culture are truly curious to hear their colleagues' points of view—particularly when they disagree on something. It sounds more like this: "Tell me more about why you think that's the right answer. I see it a different way, but you feel passionate about doing it this way, so maybe I'm missing something. Tell me more about what you see."

That's an idea-based question. That's the culture of a team that trusts each other and has respect for each other. Personality-based conflict is antagonistic. "You never take our needs into account. Don't you have any respect for my team?"

IRRATIONAL FEAR OF MAKING A MISTAKE

When a fear of failure permeates your company, progress slows to a crawl. People are afraid to try new approaches because they are worried about being second-guessed or blamed if the idea fails.

An excellent culture is not only going to accept failure but demand it. You learn from failure, and it makes you better. If you are not failing once in a while, you're probably not striving hard enough.

Sara Blakely, founder of Spanx and the first female founder of a billion-dollar private company, tells a story about how, every Sunday, her father would sit down with Sara and her brother and ask them, "What did you fail at this week?" He asked the question not because he wanted to scold them but because he knew that failing would teach them a valuable lesson. Sara said she and her brother felt like they'd screwed up if they hadn't failed at something.

If your company is afraid to try new things, if it fears failure or if it fails and doesn't admit it, that's another symptom that you've got a culture problem.

CONFUSION

Confusion and uncertainty throughout the company is a sign that your leadership team members are not having the right discussions. These situations develop, for example, when the leaders don't respect each other, don't care what their fellow leaders need, or are actively trying to make a fellow leader look bad.

Many versions of the truth lead to people running in different directions. Conflicting visions, goals, and priorities can do worse than slow you down; they can have you move backward and cause A-players to run for the doors.

DEFINING THE RIGHT CULTURE: AN ACTION PLAN

The action plan for creating a Breakthrough Leadership Team's culture encompasses three key areas:

- **Values** are a set of nonnegotiable behaviors that anchor the company's culture.

- **Vision** is a clear picture of the desired, positive future for the company.

- **Vulnerability** explores the importance of trust, commitment, and accountability on the leadership team.

The onus for creating a great culture for a leadership team falls entirely on the CEO or leader of the team. It's every leadership team member's responsibility to contribute, but the leader is accountable for setting the tone for the team. Leaders must understand how vital a Breakthrough Leadership Team is to their company's overall and continued success. Leaders who are only interested in getting the work done every day and profess they're "not good at the culture stuff" need to rethink their priorities.

The CEO is the model for the leadership team and the entire organization. If the CEO is not living the core values, not communicating the vision of the company frequently and consistently, or not promoting vulnerability-based trust (discussed in the "Vulnerability" section later in this chapter), that will cascade down through the company and affect performance.

It's also the leader's role to ensure they are forming, tweaking, and rebuilding their leadership team to create this kind of culture. First and foremost, they must bring on new people who will be a great fit, and they have to find ways to remove those who aren't (more on that in Chapter 6, "Developing and Improving Your Team").

VALUES

Core values, as we mentioned briefly in the last chapter, are a handful of nonnegotiable rules that your organization lives by. Your core values define *how* you conduct business. Typically, a company has four to six core values.

These are rules of behavior that anchor your culture. They describe what's best, what's right, and what's most noble about your organization. They are behaviors that you communicate, reinforce, and model every day. You also use them in your hiring process to ensure you hire people who live your core values. Core values are not aspirational; they are not behaviors or actions you strive for but are standards for behaviors and actions you expect everyone in the organization to follow, starting, of course, with your leadership team.

Every company has a set of core values. For some, they're unwritten but nevertheless part of the culture. For these companies, values evolve from how the company's leaders and employees habitually act. These unwritten core values are not what most of us would consider a value either. For these companies, one of their unwritten but frequently practiced core values might be "Whoever yells the loudest wins," or "Hide your mistakes so no one notices."

The best companies say, "Let's understand who we are. Let's take our best characteristics and boil them down to create a set of values that define how we work. What's best, right, and most noble about who we are?"

After they define it, they write it down and come up with stories and examples so customers, partners, and employees fully understand it. They coach the values, reward those who exemplify the values, and hire based on it.

THE THREE TESTS OF A CORE VALUE

We'll talk in a minute about an exercise for identifying your company's core values. But in the meantime, it's essential to know the three tests that determine if something is a bona fide core value or just an empty phrase that sounds good but isn't meaningful. Here are the three tests:

- **Are you committed to firing someone who blatantly and repeatedly violates a core value?** For example, you're a marketing company, and you've determined that creativity is a core value. That makes sense; successful marketing requires a degree of creativity, so you'd want to make sure your company is rich in creative minds. But what about the accounts-payable clerk in the finance division of that company? Do you expect creativity from that person? What if they do an impeccable job of paying the company's bills but are not especially creative? Would you fire them for not being creative? If the answer is no, creativity is not one of your core values.

- **Are you willing to take a financial hit to uphold this core value?** Let's say one of your company's core values is respect. You treat everyone like grandma; you respect their knowledge and experience. You would never say anything to a customer or vendor that you wouldn't say to your beloved grandmother. What if your top salesperson doesn't embrace this value? That salesperson is responsible for 35 percent of your revenue, but they treat everyone more like a servant than a grandmother. If your company is willing to put up with that behavior rather than risk 35 percent of its revenue, then treating everyone like grandma is not a core value.

- **Is this core value alive in your organization today?** If that value is not already embraced and routinely exhibited in your company, then that core value is aspirational. If it's something you hope to be but are not today, then it's not a core value. I know it's tempting to create a core value that defines who you want to be rather than who you are. The problem is that it's impossible for a core value to be both nonnegotiable (see the first two tests of a core value) and aspirational. If it's okay to not live a core value today (if it's aspirational, many won't be living it today), the whole idea of core values becomes, at best, just a plaque on the wall, or at worst, a joke. If there's a way you'd like everyone in the organization to behave that's aspirational, you can add it as a competency in everyone's job scorecard (discussed in Chapter 2, "Structuring Your Leadership Team"), set a goal to achieve it, or make it part of your vivid vision (discussed later in this chapter). But it's not a core value.

CREATE YOUR CORE VALUES

There are many ways to discover your company's core values. However, my go-to method is the Mars Group exercise described by Jim Collins, business author of *Good to Great*. This exercise should be done as a group by the leadership team. Here are the key steps:

1. Each leader on the team picks five employees to be included in a fictitious trip to Mars. The Martians don't speak English, so the mission is to show them through action what's best, right, and noble about your organization. The people you pick should be those who best exemplify what's great about your company.

2. For the five people each leader has selected, the leader must write down one or two characteristics that convinced them to pick this person for the mission. You picked Jim because of Jim's attention to detail. You picked Jill because she's so warm and caring. You picked Ezra because he works his butt off to find answers.

3. The leaders then transfer each characteristic to a Post-it Note. These Post-it Notes are put on a flip chart so all characteristics are visible to the group.

4. A facilitator (typically a coach or the CEO), with the help of the group, organizes the Post-its into groups of similar ideas. For example, "trustworthy" and "honest" might be grouped together. "Productive" and "efficient" might go together.

5. Once the characteristics are arranged in groups of similar ideas, the group takes each set of characteristics through the three tests. Most of the characteristics cited are going to fail one of the tests. Other characteristics are going to float to the top and be identified as potential core values.

6. The team then needs to discuss and debate it down to the most important three to six. One person then takes ownership for wordsmithing the values and crafting descriptions and some example stories that bring the core values to life so they can be communicated to the entire organization.

MAROTTA PLASTIC SURGERY: SAMPLE CORE VALUES

Here is an example of the core values for one of my clients. The core values are in bold face, followed by the descriptions and example stories the company uses to explain the core value.

Core Value #1: Patient-Centric Model

Following a patient-centric model means that we:

- Put the patient first
- Welcome our patients and make them feel like family
- Go out of our way to treat patients like VIPs (important)
- Treat each and every patient with kindness and respect
  - Don't judge their decisions or how they look
  - Don't talk about them behind their back
  - Try to stand in their shoes and consider how you would want to be treated
  - Go above and beyond for people and make their day

Core Value #2: Attitude Is Everything!

Adopting a positive attitude means:

- Be a leader and strive to set a positive tone in the office—have an infectious attitude
- Be passionate about what you're doing
- Squash negative chatter—don't engage in it and don't tolerate it

- Strive to be your best self
- Be open-minded and willing to change
- Set out to start each day with a sense of enthusiasm
- See the good in others
- Choose kindness

Core Value #3: Commitment to Care

Our commitment to care means:

- Following procedure and protocols for safety
- Reporting adverse events and admitting mistakes, even when it's scary to do so
  - Our goal is not to reprimand—it is to solve the problem, learn from our mistakes, and move forward, taking steps so that it doesn't happen again
  - Fix problems if something goes wrong in a manner that puts the patient's needs and well-being first
  - Keep coworkers safe
  - Create a safe environment

Core Value #4: Team Players Are A-Players

Being an A-player means:

- Being willing to pitch in when needed—having the "I can do it" attitude
- Recognizing that no job is too small

- If you see something that needs to be done, don't wait for someone else to do it—just do it!
- Keep the practice looking its best
  - If Dr. M can take out the trash, so can you!
- Be reliable and trustworthy
- Ask yourself:
  - Am I the type of coworker that other employees like to be around?
  - Do I add to the work environment or detract from it?
  - Would I want myself as a coworker/employee?
- Have respect for each other as coworkers—don't talk negatively about one another or the practice as a whole
- Be direct if you have a problem: go to your supervisor, not another staff member

VISION

A Breakthrough Leadership Team must align around a compelling vision of the future that drives them to greatness and inspires the rest of the organization. It answers the question, What will it look like when we're great? This vision, along with your core values, acts as a compass to guide the company in the right direction. When the organization is confronted with a difficult decision, it should ask itself two questions: What decision would better help us live our core values? What decision would bring us closer to our vision?

In this section, we'll describe several elements of a powerful vision. There are a number of ways to discover, clarify, and communicate your vision, but the ones I start with are:

- Core purpose

- Big Hairy Audacious Goal (BHAG)

- Three-year vision

DEFINE YOUR CORE PURPOSE

A core purpose answers the question, Why does our business exist?

It's not "To make money"—despite what your CFO says. Your purpose needs to have a higher intention than money. Money is the benefit you get for adding some value to society. What value are you adding?

For example, Disney's core purpose isn't to make movies or operate amusement parks. Disney's purpose is to make people happy. Starbucks's purpose isn't to sell coffee. Starbucks instead strives to provide people a "third place"—a welcoming environment that's neither home nor work, where you can escape the routine.

Having a core purpose gives your company something to rally behind. It gives your organization a reason for doing what it's doing. Back when I was first starting my career, I was motivated by money, status, and ascending the corporate ladder. Most people today want a grander reason for what they're doing. If they don't believe in the purpose, they're not going to do it. They need to believe they're adding value to society.

It's also important to note that your core purpose is not a goal you achieve, it's something you live every day. It's like the North Star in that, while you never actually reach it, it gives you direction. For instance, my core purpose is to help as many people as possible feel fulfilled by how they make a living. I won't wake up one day and say, "I did it! Everyone in the world now feels totally fulfilled by how they make a living!" I certainly have attainable goals as well. But my purpose drives me and inspires me, whether I'm reaching my goals or not.

A group of senators toured NASA in the sixties not long after President John F. Kennedy announced a goal of putting a man on the moon. The senators visited different departments, asking people what they were working on. "I'm building the jet propulsion system," one person said. "I'm working on the fuel line," said another. Then a guy came by with a broom, and a senator asked him what his job was. You might expect the guy to think he was being teased, but that's not how he reacted. "I'm helping put a man on the moon," the janitor said proudly. Do you think he might be a bit more motivated to do his job than if he viewed his purpose as sweeping floors?

That's why a core purpose is essential.

People in your company need to be able to see beyond the day-to-day grind of dealing with a demanding customer or whatever challenge they face. They need to see beyond that frustration and be able to say, "You know what? There's a higher purpose here. There's a reason why I'm doing this."

If you work for a company making mounting bolts, it may not seem like exciting or inspirational work—unless you know that your mounting bolts go into a type of brake used on kids' bicycles. Knowing this, you no longer think your job is about making one identical mounting bolt after another. Your whole purpose is to keep kids safe. Do you think differently about those mounting bolts now? Does that purpose put your day-to-day frustrations or boredom into a different context?

An Exercise: The Five Whys

There are many ways to discover your company's core purpose. However, my go-to method is called the Five Whys. This exercise should be done as a group by the leadership team. Here are the key steps:

The first step is for everyone on the leadership team to write down what the company does. Everyone on the team might write something like, "We design and sell supply-chain software." That's what you do. It's not your core purpose.

Ask, "Why is that important?" And then, for each answer you get, you continue to ask the same question. Here's what that might look like:

- *What do we do?* We design supply-chain software.

- *Why is that important?* Manufacturers need it to manage their inventory.

- *Why is that important?* They need it to prevent waste and increase profit.

- *Why is that important?* The manufacturing sector has struggled in the face of foreign competition, and our product makes manufacturers more competitive.

- *Why is that important?* A strong manufacturing sector creates well-paying jobs throughout the country, keeps factories operating, and helps the GNP.

- *Why is that important?* It's good for the US economy and good for Americans. It provides tax revenue that keeps schools open and public parks and services operating.

By about the fourth or fifth *why* question, you've homed in on something that makes people proud and inspired. This starts to look more like a core purpose. You're not just selling software. You're keeping an American economic institution alive, strengthening workers and communities in the process. This resonates. This is why I get up in the morning.

The next two steps involve asking two additional questions.

- **What would be lost if the company ceased to exist?** I pause and let each leader document their answer.

- How could we frame the purpose of this organization so that if you woke up tomorrow morning with enough money in the bank to retire, you would nevertheless keep working here? In other words, **What deeper sense of purpose would motivate you to continue to dedicate your precious creative energies to this company's efforts?**

Ask each leader to review their answers to each of the questions in steps 2 and 3 to determine which answer, or combination of answers, resonates with them as a potential core purpose. Then ask each leader to write down this potential core purpose on a Post-it Note and place it up on a flip chart.

A facilitator (typically a coach or the CEO), with the help of the group, organizes the Post-its into groups of similar ideas. Some will be similar, but all five or six—depending on how many people are on your team—might be different. At this point, you discuss and debate to decide which one really resonates.

The team then discusses and debates to gain agreement on

the core purpose or, at least, a directional answer for now. One person on the team then needs to take ownership of wordsmithing the purpose and bringing it back to the leadership team for approval.

I advise the companies I work with to not worry about making that core purpose statement perfect from the start. Make it good enough and then continue working on it over the next couple of months to socialize it internally, get feedback, and reword as needed. Once you feel like you've got it, the last step is to come up with a plan to communicate the core purpose to the entire organization.

The "Just Cause" Test

What we call "core purpose" here is what Simon Sinek, the author of *Start with Why* and *The Infinite Game,* calls a "just cause." In *The Infinite Game,* Sinek describes your just cause as the thing that motivates you and your employees to get out of bed and go to work with eagerness and conviction. Your just cause is what keeps you and your organization pushing ahead despite setbacks or instability. Sinek believes a just cause must be:

- **For something.** A just cause articulates what you stand for; it's not about what you are opposed to. It presents an optimistic and specific view of the future.

- **Inclusive.** It's open to anyone who wants to chip in, including investors, clients, or the community. It inspires people from diverse backgrounds, who feel welcome to contribute.

- **Service-oriented.** Its primary focus is to help others, not to merely make money or satisfy shareholders. If you invest, your primary goal should be to help the organization you are investing in, not to strictly serve your own financial interests. You should expect a return on your investment, but that should not be your primary goal.

- **Resilient.** Your just cause must be capable of surviving disruption, whether it's political, cultural, or technological.

- **Idealistic.** This characteristic is where the infinite part of Sinek's game comes into play. Your just cause should be a vision, not a goal, and it should be lofty, noble, and inspiring. It's not about hitting a revenue target or achieving a high ranking in your industry. Instead, your just cause should be unattainable—something that lives on and inspires you in the long run.

Once you've established your core purpose, these five qualities are a great way to test that purpose. If they meet all five of Sinek's characteristics, you have a strong core purpose to guide your company.

CREATE A BIG HAIRY AUDACIOUS GOAL

"All companies have goals. But there is a difference between merely having a goal and becoming committed to a huge, daunting challenge—like a big mountain to climb."

That's an excerpt from *Built to Last* by Jim Collins and Jerry Porras. They called this goal the "Big Hairy Audacious Goal" or BHAG for short. A BHAG is your ten- to thirty-year flag on top of the mountain. It's designed to challenge your organization to greatness while reinforcing business fundamentals. Your core purpose is something you live; your BHAG is something you strive to accomplish.

An example of a great BHAG was Kennedy's pronouncement in 1961 that the US would put a man on the moon by the end of the decade. When JFK announced this after Russia launched its Sputnik satellite, many scientists and engineers thought he was crazy. But it challenged the scientific minds to think outside of the box and pursue a solution. It challenged our country to greatness and helped us focus as a country on supporting the work of our space program. It was something people could rally around and get excited about.

The defining characteristic of a BHAG is that it feels nearly impossible to accomplish. If someone says, "Yeah, I could see how we can accomplish that," then your BHAG is not ambitious enough. For example, when Starbucks was working on its BHAG, it initially considered a goal of establishing thousands of locations. Jim Collins challenged them to be bolder. He said that kind of BHAG would only compel the company to keep doing what it was already doing. It wasn't going to challenge Starbucks to greatness.

As a result, Starbucks aimed higher and decided its BHAG would be to become the number one consumer brand on the planet. That's why, if you go to a baseball game, you can buy Starbucks coffee. When you go to the grocery store, you can buy Starbucks ice cream. That's why Starbucks's logo has no words on it; if you're going to be the number one consumer brand on the planet, you need a logo that is going to be the same in every country. This BHAG worked because it challenged Starbucks to greatness and gave its employees a long-term goal to rally around.

Find Your BHAG

BHAGs emerge when you locate the place where the answers to three key questions intersect:

- What are you deeply passionate about?

- What can you be the best in the world at?

- What drives your economic engine?

Fig. 13

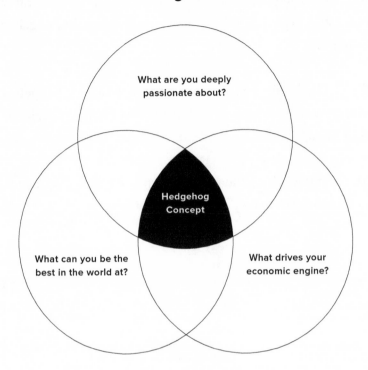

Collins calls the intersection of these circles the "hedgehog concept" (Figure 13). In Isaiah Berlin's famous essay "The Hedgehog and the Fox," Berlin says "Foxes pursue many ends at the same time and see the world in all its complexity. They are scattered or diffused, moving on many levels.... The hedgehog simplifies a complex world into a single organizing idea, the basic principle or concept that unifies and guides everything." Berlin is referring to the way a hedgehog protects itself from a predator. Regardless of whether the predator attacks from above, the side, or the front, the hedgehog reacts in the same way: by curling itself up in a ball and using its impenetrable outer shell to protect itself. This action works for the hedgehog every time.

Jim Collins's research identified that maintaining hedgehog discipline over a long period of time will help you achieve your BHAG.

According to Collins, there are four types of BHAGs. See Figure 14 for examples to help stimulate your thinking.

Fig. 14

BHAG Type	Examples
Target BHAG	By 2022, we will have delivered 10 million customers to the businesses that we service. (Red Balloon, early 2000s)
Common Enemy BHAG	Crush Adidas. (Nike, 1960s)
Role Model BHAG	Be the Harvard of coaching organizations. (Gravitas International Coaches 2019)
Internal Transformation BHAG	Transform this company from a defense contractor into the best diversified high-technology company in the world. (Rockwell, 1955)

When I work with a leadership team on BHAGs, I ask them to imagine that it's fifteen years from now. The *New York Times* or the *Wall Street Journal* has written an article about your company and some amazing thing that you just accomplished. The headline of that article is your BHAG.

As with the core values, I have the leadership team break out their Post-it Note pads and write down what they imagine that headline to say. Then the Post-its all go on the wall and the team guts it out to arrive at their BHAG.

It takes time to get it right, so don't expect your first BHAG to be the final one you select. Sometimes leadership teams—even great ones—come up with a BHAG that they think is perfect. Then, six months later, they say, "That was dumb. We're not going to do that. We're going to do this instead."

That's okay. It's not supposed to be an easy exercise. Some leaders are skilled tacticians, and they know what to execute and when. But when it comes to stepping back and thinking strategically in this way, they can struggle. The idea is that you evolve your BHAG over the next several months until you get it right. When everyone feels good about it, you roll it out to the entire organization and start measuring your progress toward reaching that goal.

Although the BHAG is a long way off and should be almost mind-bogglingly difficult, it nevertheless creates a sense of urgency in your company. It keeps your goals from being too pedestrian, too easy. It's also a great way to attract outstanding employees who share this passion and want to be part of an effort to reach this inspiring place.

As with your core values and core purpose, the only way to keep your BHAG foremost on your company's mind is to communicate it, communicate it, and communicate it again. You can't tell people about it once and assume they're going to be excited and stay that way. You have to reinforce the idea. When someone in your company does something extraordinary, you don't just pat them on the back and say, "Good job." Instead, you pat them on the back and say, "That amazing accomplishment brings us closer to our BHAG."

Again, you should use your core values, core purpose, and BHAG in your decision-making process. If you aren't sure which option to choose, ask yourself, "Which of these choices moves us closer to our BHAG? Which option is more in line with our core values? Which option helps us better live our core purpose?"

Everyone in your company needs an Everest-like goal that they can stay focused on. The value of a BHAG is that it's so audacious that people will not debate you about it. In contrast, if you set a five-year goal of doubling revenue, people will line up to either tell you that you'll never reach that level in such a short time frame or that you can do much better than that. When

Paul Allen and Bill Gates started Microsoft thirty years ago, no one challenged their BHAG of putting a personal computer on every desk in every home.

CREATE YOUR THREE-YEAR VISION

Core values, core purpose, and BHAG are long-term, foundational elements of a company's strategy and vision that almost never change. I believe a shorter-term, three-year vision is critical as well to ensure your leadership team is aligned and that each member is a true believer, supporter, and evangelist of the vision. The three-year vision also provides the link between your long-term vision and your day-to-day execution.

I use two specific tools with my clients to create their three-year vision. There are great books written on both, so I won't try to reproduce both processes here. What follows is a short description of each. I highly recommend you read both books for more details.

Vivid Vision

In his book *Vivid Vision*, Cameron Herold advises leaders to write a description of what their company will look like in three years.

> When I walk through the front door of our offices, the level of energy is amazing. We just doubled our revenue again. We've got

pictures of happy clients on the walls. Every conference room is filled with people working together on new products. The media is saying we have once again been voted the best place to work in our community.

This vivid vision imagines what your company looks like, smells like, and feels like three years in the future.

3HAG

The term 3HAG stands for three-year highly achievable goal. It was coined by Shannon Byrne Susko in her book, *3HAG WAY: The Strategic Execution System That Ensures Your Strategy Is Not a Wild-Ass Guess!* The three-year highly achievable goal is a strategic execution system that builds confidence in your ability to predict future growth and make it happen. It's important because it links strategy with execution. Instead of a five-year, wild-ass guess, it allows you to tie your three-year highly achievable goal to your BHAG (in the long term) and your 1HAG (in the short term). The 3HAG is the glue between your day-to-day execution and your BHAG. It uses strategic pictures that allow you to better visualize your strategy with the team and review or tweak that strategy on a regular basis. The major focus is on creating three-year targets (revenue, gross margin, net profit, number of units sold, etc.), and three-year actions that differentiate you in your marketplace.

VULNERABILITY

The word "vulnerability" typically has a negative connotation. In fact, here's one definition I found online at Lexico.com: "The quality or state of being exposed to the possibility of being attacked or harmed, either physically or emotionally." That doesn't sound like fun. However, vulnerability is critical on a Breakthrough Leadership Team. On a Breakthrough Leadership Team, being vulnerable means a willingness to admit when you've made a mistake or don't know how to do something. Vulnerability is also a willingness to give and receive honest feedback without fear of retribution and a willingness to subvert your needs to the needs of the team.

In this section, I'll describe vulnerability-based trust and accountability.

DEVELOP VULNERABILITY-BASED TRUST

According to Patrick Lencioni in his book *The Five Dysfunctions of a Team*, the lack of vulnerability-based trust is the foundational dysfunction on most teams. Put in a more positive way, vulnerability-based trust is the foundational characteristic of any cohesive team. We're not talking about task-based trust—such as when you trust that another team member will do the task they agreed to do. That's important, but it doesn't build a culture.

Vulnerability-based trust allows team members to be open and honest, even when the topic might be scary or uncomfortable. It's the kind of trust that allows a team member to say, "I'm not sure I know what to do and need some help," or "I made a mistake, and now I'm not sure I can meet our target date." They show vulnerability—even though it hurts a little bit—and the result is that the rest of the team trusts you more and will likely show their vulnerability because you were willing to open up. In his book *The Culture Code*, Daniel Coyle explains that the "vulnerability loop" has some distinct steps:

1. Person A sends a signal of vulnerability. "I'm sorry I missed that deadline. The work was harder than I thought."

2. Person B detects the signal of vulnerability.

3. Person B responds by signaling their own vulnerability. "I had a similar problem last year on a different project. It made me feel terrible."

4. Person A detects the signal from Person B.

5. A new norm emerges and closeness and trust increase. By being open and honest, Person A enables Person B to be the same way. Trust—and the willingness to be more open and honest in the future—is the result.

Conduct the Personal Lifeline Exercise

One way to quickly develop vulnerability-based trust on a leadership team is to encourage people to share more about their lives, both professional and personal. I use a great exercise from *Terrific Training Techniques for Career Development Practitioners* by Judy Kaplan Baron. It's called the Personal Lifeline.

Here's the process:

1. Start with each person drawing a horizontal line across a blank sheet of paper. The left-hand edge of the line is the day they were born, and the right-hand side is today.

2. Each member of the leadership team then marks on that lifeline the eight or ten major high points and low points in their life. These can be school experiences, births, the death of a parent, a marriage, job changes, or any other major milestones in their life. Each person notes the highlights above the lifeline and the lowlights below the line. The position (high or low) of that mark should equate to the intensity of that experience

3. Once they've marked their experiences, each person puts a plus sign (+) next to the best decision they ever made, a negative sign (-) next to the worst decision, an exclamation point (!) next to the greatest risk they took, and a zero (0) next to a critical decision that was made for you by someone else.

4. Once everyone has completed their lifeline, go around the table so each person can present their lifeline and describe the events it depicts.

If your team already has some vulnerability-based trust, it's not unusual for these presentations to get emotional. I don't think I've ever done it without someone getting choked up or coming close to tears. I remember one participant, an executive in his late thirties, who broke down when he talked about his parents' divorce when he was a kid. It still packed an emotional wallop for him.

Although the process can be a little painful, the benefits are far-reaching. Team members begin to understand each other at a much deeper level and build a much greater level of trust.

I recommend that a leadership team do this exercise any time a new member joins the team. When you bring someone new onto the leadership team, you're changing the dynamic of that leadership team. It's almost like you now have a new team, so that vulnerability-based trust needs to be revisited and practiced.

Conduct the "I'm Sorry" or "I Need Help" Exercise

In this group exercise, each leader is asked to either say, "I'm sorry," to another leader in the room who they feel they owe an apology or ask the group, or an individual, for help dealing with a challenge they haven't been able to resolve on their own. No one gets a pass; each person either has to say, "I'm sorry," to someone, or "I need help," to someone else on the team.

It's amazing how this simple exercise opens the team up, heals wounds, and sparks really important conversations. It challenges people to mend a relationship that might be frayed or to admit when they erred. It challenges people to not try to be the hero but to admit in front of everyone that they need help.

INJECT ACCOUNTABILITY

One of the big challenges I hear from leaders all the time is, "I can't seem to find a way to hold my team accountable." However, it's not solely the job of the CEO to hold the leadership team accountable. It's a leadership team's job to hold each other accountable.

Leaders on a Breakthrough Leadership Team are willing to be held accountable to the commitments they make and are willing to hold others on the team accountable as well. If the head of sales didn't meet his goals, you don't sit around waiting for the leader to scold the head of sales. As a member of the team, you have the right to say, "We were counting on you, Sales. You committed, and you didn't come through. What can we do to prevent this in the future?"

Without true accountability, discipline dies. Lack of accountability has a devastating impact on an organization.

First, lack of accountability breeds frustration throughout the organization as team members learn they can't rely on each other. This has a dramatic impact on morale and trust within the organization, bringing productivity down and making it harder to recruit A-players.

Second, and most importantly, lack of accountability leads to stagnation. As the frustration grows, people give up and stop making commitments. They say things like, "Priorities are just changing too fast for me to make a commitment," or "Why should I care if I miss a deadline if no one is going to follow up anyway?" This is a death toll for a growing organization.

There are many reasons for this challenge, but the first is that most organizations don't really know the difference between accountability and responsibility. Here are some key distinctions.

- **Responsibility**—The job of the person responsible is to roll up their sleeves and get the job done. Responsibility can be assigned to one person or a group of people. It's perfectly accurate to say something like, "We're all responsible for customer service in this organization."

- **Accountability**—Accountability is always and only one person. The person accountable owns the result, but they're not necessarily the person doing the work. While they can't delegate their accountability away, they can absolutely delegate responsibility. The person accountable needs to ensure there's a plan, and they need to ensure the right measures are in place to gauge success or failure.

The CEO of one of my clients consistently complained to me that his team was not following through on their commitments. However, when I asked if he had followed through on a few things he had committed to, he gave me a list of excuses. It's not surprising that his leadership team followed his example.

The CEO and the leadership team need to set the tone. They need to be willing to hold themselves accountable by honoring commitments and owning up when they haven't. If they provide a poor example of accountability, the rest of the organization will follow their lead.

A culture of accountability is about clarity. Say what you mean and mean what you say.

Know Your #1 Team

When I start working with a company, its leadership team often doesn't have much of an identity. The leadership team is a bunch of people that happen to report to the CEO. They meet occasionally to talk about their work but don't really act like, or feel like, a team.

If they are honest, these leaders will tell you that they are most loyal to their own teams and not to the leadership team. The head of finance will say his #1 team is his finance department. The head of sales will say he's tightest with the sales team and so forth. What's more, in most companies, these leaders are focused more on their own team's goals than on the company's goals. The head of sales says, "I'm doing my job. We're out there selling and hitting our goals. The fact that the company is not shipping correctly or that our product quality is inconsistent or that customers complain about our service department, those aren't my problems."

But in great companies with Breakthrough Leadership Teams, each member of the leadership team is focused on the company's goals to a greater degree than their own goals. Their #1 team is always the leadership team. Their #1 goal is to make the leadership team successful. Everything else is secondary. That means the head of sales is prepared to subordinate the sales divisions' needs and goals to help operations solve a problem if that's a higher priority for the leadership team. That means service is willing to jump in and help sales if revenues are down and turning around the top line is the highest priority for the leadership team. For all the leaders in the company, the leadership team must be the highest priority and the #1 team.

Disagree and Commit

A culture based on core values, vision, and vulnerability allow team members to "disagree and commit." This is a term Patrick

Lencioni, in his book *The Five Dysfunctions of a Team* (you can tell how much I like that book based on how many times I've referred to it), uses to describe how a team may have heated debates, but when the discussion is over and a decision is made, everyone on the leadership team commits fully to the team's agreement.

Disagree and commit starts with idea-based conflict, as opposed to the personality-based conflict we discussed in the "Symptoms of a Weak Culture" section. Idea-based conflict, even if it gets emotional, is a good thing. It's each member of the team's job to debate and challenge each other's ideas to ensure all sides of an issue are explored. As Lencioni once said in a speech I attended, "If you don't get productive conflict right, based on ideas, then that fear of conflict actually ferments into personality-based conflict."

Once a decision is made, even if you fought passionately for a different approach, you need to be as committed as anyone else at the table to making the decision work. You don't leave the meeting and tell your subordinates, "Well, they went with the option I was opposed to. I lost that battle. We'll have to make the best of it." That's what most people do, but that's not disagree and commit. "Making the best of it" results in a team that's looking for every excuse to prove it was the wrong decision.

Disagree and commit is when, as a member of your leadership team, you go back to your subordinates and say, "As a leadership team, we decided this was the best option. Let's talk about how we're going to make it work." No "making the best of it." No "I was opposed to it." As a leader, you can argue vehemently for your point of view. But once you have been heard and a decision is made, you must, as a member of the leadership team, commit to making it work.

Conduct the Peer Accountability Exercise

I use a simple but effective exercise twice a year to develop greater accountability on a leadership team. This exercise develops the muscles required to hold fellow team members accountable for their contributions to the team. It also develops the muscles needed to receive feedback without being defensive. This exercise was inspired by Lencioni in *The Five Dysfunctions of a Team.*

Fig. 15

OTHERS

Name	They Should Keep Doing...	They Should Change...

Fig. 16

YOU

Name	You Should Keep Doing...	You Should Change...

What 1-2 behaviors do you plan to work on immediately?

_____

_____

_____

The exercise requires that each team member gives their fellow leadership team members feedback on what they do that brings great value to the team and what they do that hurts the team (see Figures 15 and 16). Here are the critical steps:

1. **Decide on the feedback you'll be giving to your fellow team members.** Each member of the leadership team writes the names of the other members of the leadership team in the first column of the Peer Accountability Exercise template (Figure 15). After each name, there are two columns.

   In the first column, you write down the one most important thing that team member does regularly that helps the team. It could be the fresh ideas they bring or the way they ask revealing questions as examples. Whatever that quality or behavior is, it brings tremendous value to the team, and you want that team member to keep doing it.

   In the second column, you write down the one most important thing each person is doing to hurt the team. Maybe they judge others too quickly or fail to listen carefully to others' ideas. Whatever it is, it is the most significant way the team member distracts or subtracts from the group's work.

2. **Form a circle.** After the group is finished filling out their forms, I have them leave the meeting table and put their chairs in a circle so there is nothing between them and the

other team members. I find that this arrangement helps ensure that everyone is open, honest, and not defensive. There is something about sitting in a circle without a table in front of them that allows a group to go a little deeper in its conversation.

3. **Review the positive feedback.** I always start with feedback for the CEO. We'll go around the circle, and one by one, each team member will tell the CEO what he or she does that is indispensable to the team's success. They describe the most critical thing the CEO does that adds value to the team, and they thank the CEO and ask them to please continue behaving in this effective way.

    Here's an important rule: when the CEO (or any member of the group) is getting his or her feedback, they can have only one of two responses. He or she can either say, "Thank you," or ask a question if they are unclear or don't understand the feedback. That's it. There is no other response—no heavy sighs, jokes, or defensiveness. There is no agreement or disagreement. The CEO should be taking notes on each piece of feedback. (See Figure 16 for an example.)

4. **Move on to areas of improvement.** Once we've gone around the circle, and everyone has given the CEO their positive feedback, we switch gears and go around the loop again. This time, each team member tells the leader what he or she is doing or not doing that hurts the team. The leader

gets some hard feedback, but again, the only response is "Thank you" or a clarifying question. There isn't any debate or defensiveness. The leader does not get to challenge the assessment or disagree with it. As soon as someone gets defensive and says something like, "I don't see myself that way," the whole process gets shut down. No one is going to want to give you feedback if you aren't willing to accept it. Again, the leader should be taking notes on each piece of feedback.

5. **Follow the same process for each team member.** Once the leader has received all of his or her feedback, follow the same process with the next person. As we go around the circle, the person receiving feedback uses the form (Figure 16) to take notes on what they are hearing.

6. **Reflect and commit.** Once everyone has received their feedback, each person takes a few minutes to review their notes. They are looking for one or two things that they will commit to doing differently in the future. Then we go around the circle again, and each team member identifies the most important one to two actions or behaviors they are committing to change based on the feedback. If the leader heard three people say that he hurts the team when he interrupts people, one of his actions might be, "I'm going to be more patient so people can finish making their point."

When a team performs an exercise like this, it allows team members to hold each other accountable for the changes they're committing to make. The next time the leader interrupts someone on the team, the team member feels comfortable pointing out the unfortunate behavior. "Hey Joe, remember two weeks ago when we did that peer accountability exercise and you vowed to stop interrupting people? Well, you just did it again." The leader at this point is free to smile sheepishly, do a palm slap to the forehead, or turn the imaginary key that locks his lips, and the discussion continues.

When to Do the Peer Accountability Exercise

This is a powerful exercise, but it only works effectively with teams that already have a high level of trust and safety. With new teams or teams where members don't feel comfortable with each other, people are afraid to be honest. Instead, they will try not to hurt anyone's feelings and will give each other hollow feedback that isn't helpful. And, of course, the exercise fails the second someone gets defensive, angry, or accusatory.

How do you know if your team is ready for this exercise? There is no hard and fast clue, but if you see your team members being honest and open in their regular work, they are probably ready. However, if there are a lot of private, closed-door meetings where buddies on the leadership team complain about someone else on the team, your team is not ready for this exercise. If you see defensive behavior or personality conflicts on the team, this exercise isn't going to help improve the situation.

It's helpful to have an outside facilitator conduct the exercise the first few times you do it. However, if the team understands the process, they can do the exercise without one. No matter how many times you've done it, it's critical to remind everyone of the ground rules—you can either say thank you or ask a clarifying question. It's also critical to cut off any discussions that might veer off target or bog the process down. But most of the time when I do this exercise, I lay out the ground rules, and the process unfolds without any wrinkles.

It's also vital to start with the CEO. When I conduct this exercise with a client, I usually meet ahead of time with the CEO to discuss how it works and to emphasize how crucial their behavior is. The CEO must be a model for how to accept the feedback; if the CEO disrupts the process, then no one will take it seriously.

Most teams are a little nervous the first time I suggest they do the exercise. They'll hem and haw and claim not to be familiar enough with a person's performance. I don't buy that. I tell them that they *do* know how someone contributes to or hurts the team and that they owe it to their team and to their members to help them get better. If you're going to have a Breakthrough Leadership Team, you need to be totally committed to helping each other improve.

BRINGING IT ALL TOGETHER

Although it can take years to create a Breakthrough Leadership

Team—and it's an ongoing challenge to keep that team continually improving—the results can be astonishing. The culture we discussed will result in a team that has better discussions and will reach better decisions. It has conflict about the right things, and the company's values and vision will be clear. You have greater accountability and real passion and energy about carrying out the vision, and that enthusiasm seeps down and permeates all levels of the company.

The three elements of values, vision, and vulnerability cascade down from the leadership team to the entire company. Sales and service, finance and marketing—these teams are going to want to work together because the leaders at the top work together. Values cascade down because people see their leaders living those values every day. Vision cascades down because if my bosses are true believers in the vision, they will be telling stories about it and focusing on it over and over. Vulnerability cascades down because, if my leader is willing to be vulnerable, accountable, and loyal to the team, so will I.

A resulting sign that you have the right culture is when your leadership team develops camaraderie. A Breakthrough Leadership Team should like each other. Team members don't have to be best friends, but they do want to build each other up and help each other out. A good example is my favorite baseball team, the New York Yankees. As I write this, they are in first place. However, most of their best players are currently injured and have been replaced by less-skilled players from the minor leagues. But the chemistry on the team and its culture of support and camaraderie has resulted in what is basically a minor league team continuing to win and occupy first place in the American League Eastern Division. You can be a good leadership team without that culture, but if you want to be a Breakthrough Leadership Team, you need that level of camaraderie.

Keep in mind that your goal is not just to have a bunch of happy people working for you. The goal is to develop greater productivity, creativity, and growth. When you do that, you get happier employees who feel better about what they do.

Your leadership team must be far more than an all-star group of talented A-players. If the team has this glue that binds them together, you can do more with a less talented leadership team than with all-stars who don't embrace what's most important. Someone may be talented, but if they don't buy in to and live your culture, they are going to be toxic to the organization.

## CHAPTER 5

EXECUTING WITH DISCIPLINE

A great strategy executed without discipline and accountability will fail every time. If you have a good strategy but you execute the hell out of it, you will blow away the competition.

Discipline is a ritual or habit that you practice every day. It's the routine you follow to go from where you are now to where you want to be. If you exercise four days a week and eat the right food, that's a discipline that will lead you to better health. In business, discipline comprises the customs you follow and the practices you adopt to drive your company toward its objectives.

WHY YOU SHOULD CARE ABOUT DISCIPLINED EXECUTION

If your organization doesn't have any real discipline, you and all of your employees can work hard every day and still feel overwhelmed by day-to-day challenges and demands. It's hard to know if you're working smart or making any progress what-soever. The result is chaos.

Discipline takes you from chaos to predictability.

Highly successful companies execute with great discipline. Everyone understands the company's priorities, measures success the right way, communicates clearly, and runs in the same direction—toward your company's goals. Along the way, they are all talking to each other, helping each other, holding each other accountable, and teaming up to find solutions to obstacles. Companies like these are an unstoppable force.

Looking at the same study in the introduction that shows the importance of leadership buy-in and support (Figure 1), we can see that the next seven biggest reasons for the failure of a strategic initiative have to do with poor execution.

Fig. 1

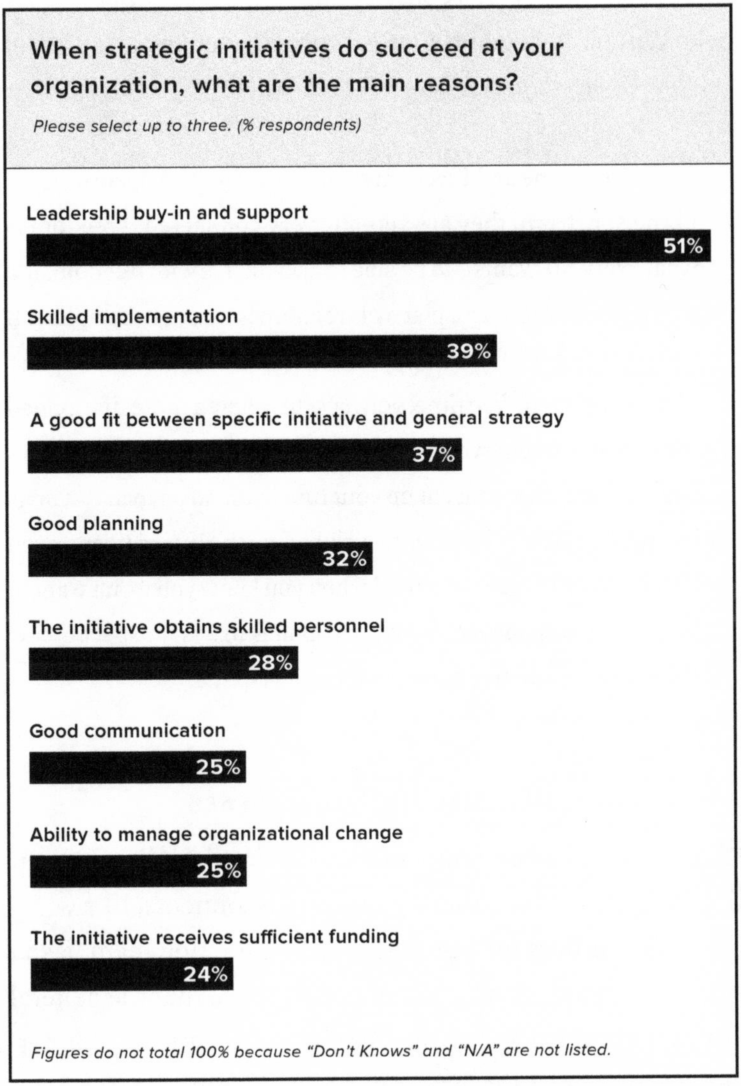

When strategic initiatives do succeed at your organization, what are the main reasons?

Please select up to three. (% respondents)

Leadership buy-in and support
51%

Skilled implementation
39%

A good fit between specific initiative and general strategy
37%

Good planning
32%

The initiative obtains skilled personnel
28%

Good communication
25%

Ability to manage organizational change
25%

The initiative receives sufficient funding
24%

Figures do not total 100% because "Don't Knows" and "N/A" are not listed.

Some hear the word "discipline" and automatically have a negative reaction. It seems constraining, but it's the opposite. As Jocko Willink, a former Navy Seal commander and coauthor of *Extreme Ownership*, states in a *Forbes* article,

> While Discipline and Freedom seem like they sit on opposite sides of the spectrum, they are actually very connected. Freedom is what everyone wants—to be able to act and live with freedom. But the only way to get to a place of freedom is through discipline. If you want financial freedom, you have to have financial discipline. If you want more free time, you have to follow a more disciplined time-management system. You also have to have the discipline to say "no" to things that eat up your time with no payback—things like random YouTube videos, click-bait on the Internet, and even events that you agree to attend when you know you won't want to be there. *Discipline equals freedom* applies to every aspect of life: if you want more freedom, get more discipline.

WHEN DISCIPLINED EXECUTION DISAPPEARS

It's easy to tell when your company lacks disciplined execution. You start to see these puzzling disconnects, like when sales takes orders for a product your production team hasn't started working on yet. Or you might notice that the general atmosphere at work feels disorganized or fractured. This happens to companies that grow quickly; suddenly, what felt like a simple business when there were just five of you sitting around the kitchen table doing the work feels helter-skelter when you have fifty, a hundred, or a thousand employees. It feels like every day brings another crisis.

Here are some warning signs.

STRESS AND CONSTANT "FIRE DRILLS"

If you and your team are constantly frustrated and stressed by problems of the moment, you have an execution problem. To paraphrase Michael Gerber from his book *The E-Myth Revisited: Why Most Small Businesses Don't Work and What to Do About It*, as a leader, if you spend most of your time "working *in* your business" (sleeves up, getting the today's work done) and very little time "working *on* your business" (thinking about, and improving the business for the future), you have an execution problem.

Without disciplined execution, each year, quarter, month, week, and day seems like a brand-new adventure. Adventures are fun for the movies, but it's pretty dangerous and stressful if that's how you run your business.

TEAMS WORKING AT CROSS PURPOSES

Another warning sign is when teams within your company have conflicting priorities. For instance, the sales team might think its foremost goal is to maximize revenue, while the product management team's goal is to maximize gross margin. Product managers aren't that interested in products that deliver very little profit—even if they sell well.

These goals sound similar, but they can actually put these two teams running in opposite directions. Sales is pushing the hot-selling widget and complains to product management when supplies run low.

"Why are we out of widgets that sell like hot cakes?" they ask. "That's bad for sales!"

The product managers give them a perplexed look. "What's the point in selling those widgets?" they respond. "There's no profit in them. Sell gizmos instead. The margins are higher."

Now you have misalignment and a battle raging between departments. The losers in that battle are your customers and, ultimately, your company and your employees.

I recently had a client who decided, as a leadership team, that they would focus on selling to large companies. When that became difficult, the sales team took it upon themselves to start focusing on small to midsized companies. This resulted in a need to bring on more customers than they planned in order to hit their revenue goals. But no one informed the service department of this change in plans. The service department was unprepared for the number of new clients, resulting in poor service and a significant decrease in client retention.

CONFUSION DUE TO LACK OF CLARITY

A leadership team's best-laid plans will yield no benefit if there is confusion or a lack of clarity of information both up and down the organization.

In a top-down scenario, the leadership team might be crystal clear on what the company's goals are, but it hasn't taken the time to explain it well to the rest of the company. Sometimes, as a sketchy message works its way down through the company, its meaning is distorted. One team heard "gross margin," but the next team heard "revenue."

In the bottom-up scenario, the leadership team thinks everything is going great, but on the shop floor, the workers are ready to leave the company because they don't like how they're being treated. That message never worked its way up to the leadership team.

Poor communication starts with murky messages. The leader, assuming everyone knows what he means, announces at a mandatory companywide meeting, "Our goal this year is growth! We're going to grow 20 percent!"

That sounds exciting! But as employees at the meeting are listening to this, some think the leader means they are increasing production by 20 percent, others think the company workforce will grow 20 percent, and others think the company will add 20 percent more customers. What the leader actually meant is that the goal is to grow *profit* by 20 percent.

The communication was there, but the clarity was not.

LACK OF SPECIFIC GOALS

What's worse is a company that has no stated goals at all. I notice this sometimes when leaders or business owners call to ask about coaching. When I ask them what their most important goal is for the next year, many of them have to think about it. They don't know. Well, if *they* don't know what the company's goal is, how are the *employees* supposed to know? Everybody may be out there working hard, but what are they trying to achieve?

When I hear this, I'm reminded of Lewis Carroll, paraphrased from *Alice's Adventures in Wonderland*: "If you don't know where you are going, any road will take you there."

Leaders without specific goals or priorities tend to assume that "everyone knows we need to grow." First, never assume people know that. Second, never assume people know how much you'd like to grow. Third, don't assume people know how you plan to grow. Fourth, don't assume people know why you want to grow.

Without specific goals, there is no finish line and no feeling of achievement.

FINGER POINTING

Some organizations get a gold medal in playing the blame game. The leader says, "We've got a revenue problem," and levels a long, cold look at the VP of sales. The VP throws up her hands and says, "It's not me! It's customer service. They're not shipping product accurately." Customer service blames finance for not funding a new conveyor system, finance blames the board, the board blames the leader, and so on.

You get the idea. You've probably seen it in action. No one takes accountability, and the problem festers as a result.

GREAT PLANS WITH NO FOLLOW THROUGH

For the first fifteen years of my career, I worked for two big consulting firms, and our clients were all Fortune 500 companies. These companies often spent millions of dollars, hired hundreds of consultants, and spent months creating their strategic plans. These plans were works of art. They had elegant Power-Points, graphs, and charts, and after the plans were printed out, they went into a binder and then sat on a shelf gathering dust.

These strategic plans failed because no one executed them. It's not that the people in the company weren't smart enough. It's not because there wasn't buy-in from leadership either. And it certainly wasn't because the plan wasn't thorough.

The reason these plans were never executed was because three to five months after they were created, the world had changed. The economy shifted. Some new technological innovation arrived on the scene. Or some new opportunity emerged that the company hadn't considered when it wrote its plan. Some of these changes were large and some were small, but they all conspired to make the strategic plan obsolete before the company could implement it. This happens in small and midsized companies too.

INCONSISTENT RESULTS

If you don't consistently hit your revenue and profit goals, that's a strong clue that you're not executing well. You can think you have great strategy, alignment, metrics, and communication, but if you keep falling short of your goals, something's off. You may have the wrong priorities. You may not be communicating the right things. Or you may not be measuring the right things.

EXECUTING WITH DISCIPLINE: AN ACTION PLAN

Disciplined execution starts with a plan. Not a plan that will be outdated after three to five months, but a living, breathing plan that's adjusted regularly in reaction to the changing business landscape.

Here's a key characteristic of the living, breathing plan: it must include shorter-term plans that you execute over the next ninety days.

Every quarter, review progress against the plan for the year and ask yourself, "What do we need to do for the next ninety days?" These ninety-day plans are what drive your one-year, three-year, or ten-year plans. Ninety days is long enough to get something meaningful done but short enough to create a sense of urgency. Strategic thinking and planning are important, but initiatives are not accomplished in ten years or three years or even one year. Things get done in ninety-day sprints.

Here's another way to look at it. If my goal is to lose twenty-five pounds over the next twelve months and someone puts a cupcake in front of me, I might say, "You know what? I've got a whole year to lose that weight. That cupcake looks good."

However, if I knew I had to lose six pounds in the next ninety days to stay on track to lose twenty-five pounds for the year, I might look at that cupcake a little differently. That cupcake is now a threat to my ninety-day weight-loss plan, so I decide to forego that sugary treat. That's how ninety-day plans, also called ninety-day sprints, keep you focused and help you make progress on your longer-term strategic goals.

You are still working your ten- to thirty-year BHAG, your three-year 3HAG, and your annual plan. But every ninety days when you are planning your sprint, you look back at those long-term plans and ask yourself these questions:

- Do our core ideologies still make sense? Do our core purpose, core values, and BHAG still drive us to greatness?

- Does our three-year plan still make sense? Is it still driving us toward our BHAG? Is it still consistent with our core purpose and core values?

- Does our one-year plan still make sense? Is it still driving us toward our three-year plan? Has anything changed internally or externally that should cause us to rethink our goals and priorities? Are there old opportunities that no longer make sense to focus on? Are there new priority opportunities that weren't on our radar before?

You are routinely reflecting on and adjusting your plans, and you're keeping your engine revved up with your ninety-day sprints.

THE THREE DISCIPLINES OF EXECUTION

Strong execution relies on three key disciplines:

- Aligning around priorities

- Measuring what matters

- Implementing a consistent planning and communication rhythm

These disciplines borrow heavily from Verne Harnish in his book *Scaling Up*, a book I contributed to back in 2014.

ALIGN AROUND PRIORITIES

Prioritization is typically one of the biggest challenges for an ambitious, well-meaning leadership team. These teams see eighteen incredible opportunities for growth and seventeen things they want to fix in their business, so they commit to attack all of those things. Here's the problem: if everything is a priority, nothing is a priority. There are never enough hours in the day to get everything done. But there are always enough hours to get the most important things done.

A Breakthrough Leadership Team must make the tough decisions about what's most important. A Breakthrough Leadership Team must get rid of the noise and select two to five most important items for the coming year. Which priorities will take precedence above all else? Which priorities will act like lead dominoes and drive us most effectively toward our vision?

Aligning priorities across different departments or divisions within a company is a must, but aligning short-term priorities to the long-term is also key. Short-term goals and execution must be in service to the long-term vision and values we discussed in Chapter 4, "Defining the Right Culture."

Let's define the three types of priorities: annual priorities, quarterly company rocks, and quarterly department rocks. We'll also discuss how to ensure you review and update those priorities regularly and how you cascade these priorities through your organization.

Define Annual Priorities

Before the beginning of each fiscal year, the leadership team must decide on the top two to five priorities for the upcoming year. We'll define "priority" to mean something your organization must accomplish to meet your financial targets and drive toward your company vision. These priorities should focus on ways to improve the business (working on the business) versus someone's day-to-day job (working in the business). These priorities should also be SMART—specific, measurable, achievable, realistically high, and time targeted.

Here are some examples of annual priorities:

- Implement a new ERP system to drive inventory turns of X and order fill of Y by the end of the year.

- Develop and implement three new service offerings that result in $750,000 in revenue by the end of the year.

- Add five new strategic alliances that result in $5 million in revenue by the end of the year.

- Implement a new coaching and employee-development process that results in an 80 percent employee net promoter score and 50 percent A-players by the end of the year.

These priorities should be defined and agreed upon by the leadership team, not by the CEO handing these down from above. These should be created in the annual planning retreat described below in the "Implement Consistent Planning and Communication Rhythms" section.

Define Quarterly Company Rocks

With annual priorities as our first execution step, we're now ready to define our quarterly priorities. We call these priorities "rocks" due to the metaphor popularized by Stephen Covey, author *of The 7 Habits of Highly Effective People.*

Imagine your time as a big bucket and your activities as rocks (most important), pebbles (less important), and sand (trivial activities). Without proper planning, your time tends to fill with the pebbles and sand, leaving little room for the big rocks. However, if you put the big rocks in first, the pebbles and sand will fill in around them. Rocks are the major things you want to accomplish, so you need to put them in the bucket first. That's why we call our most important quarterly priorities "rocks."

Like annual priorities, there should be two to five company rocks for the quarter. These rocks are typically created by crafting the next ninety-day chunk of an annual priority. For example, if our annual priority is "Implement a new ERP system to drive inventory turns of X and order fill of Y by EOY," a rock for the first quarter might be "Select a new ERP system and plan the implementation by EOQ." Also, like annual priorities, these rocks should focus on ways to improve the business (working on the business) versus someone's day-to-day job (working in the business). Working on the business is when you take a step back from the daily grind and ask yourself, "What's next? How do we take our business to the next level? How can we improve as a business?"

These quarterly rocks are typically created two to three weeks before the beginning of each quarter. Also, like annual priorities, these should be SMART—specific, measurable, achievable, realistically high, and time-targeted.

Each rock also needs someone—always just one person—who will be accountable for that rock. Even if the rock overlaps two departments, one person has to be accountable. Remember the difference between accountability and responsibility: accountability is always and only one person.

As an example, one company rock might be to double the sales force in order to reach revenue goals. Someone on the leadership team might say the head of sales should be accountable. But someone else might point out that HR will play a big role in carrying that rock because they will have to hire so many people. Even in cases like this, you can't have the head of sales and head of HR both be accountable—it has to be one or the other or someone else entirely. If you decide the head of sales will be accountable for the rock, HR will still be responsible for some heavy lifting required to make it happen.

Each rock owner should create a plan to accomplish the rock with milestones and metrics so that the leadership team is clear on what they're trying to accomplish and when so they can be held accountable.

Define Quarterly Department Rocks

In addition to company rocks, the leadership teams I coach all have department rocks which are of lesser importance than the company rocks. These department rocks might be something important that's specific to a department, like realigning sales territories to increase the number of sales meetings and sales closing ratios.

On these leadership teams, each leader is accountable for one to two rocks (one might be a company rock and one might be a department rock) each quarter. This ensures that each leader is accountable for working on the business and generating improvement each and every quarter.

Cascade Priorities throughout the Organization

After identifying your annual priorities and quarterly rocks, you must communicate these priorities to the rest of the company. This helps ensure alignment throughout the organization and discourages work on nonessential projects. Everyone in the company—clear on the company's immediate goals—concentrates on achieving those goals.

The first step in cascading priorities is communication. The second step is that everyone in the organization should be accountable for one or two rocks that align with a company rock. For example, a human resources recruiter is on the lookout for new hires to support a company rock focused on expansion. Or a marketing analyst might be focused on creating new marketing materials for a rock focused on implementing new service offerings. Not all individual rocks are aligned, but at least 50 percent should be aligned with the company rocks. If not aligned with company rocks, the individual rocks should be focused on work *on* the business, not *in* the business. You should be able to go ask anyone in the organization the following question and get an accurate and specific answer: "What are the three most important priorities for the company this quarter? What are you doing to contribute to the success of those priorities?"

Review and Update Priorities

Annual priorities should be reviewed each quarter. Are these still the right priorities to drive us toward our three-year plan? Has anything changed internally or externally that should cause us to rethink our goals and priorities? Are there old opportunities that no longer make sense to focus on? Are there new priority opportunities that weren't on our radar before?

Although quarterly rocks are created each quarter, they should be reviewed during each weekly and monthly meeting (discussed further in the section below, "Implement Consistent Planning and Communication Rhythms"). Any changes to a rock (removing it because it's no longer a priority or making major changes to it) should be discussed and agreed upon by the leadership team. When team members regularly change their rocks without leadership team discussions, any sense of accountability dies, and confusion awaits.

MEASURE WHAT MATTERS: KEY PERFORMANCE INDICATORS

Imagine watching a sporting event, and no one was keeping score. Things would get boring very quickly. It would seem more like a practice than a game. People need to know the score. People need to know if they (and the company) are "winning the game."

The best way to measure your progress is by using key performance indicators (KPIs). Two types of KPIs that help us keep score are lagging and leading indicators.

- **Lagging indicators**—Most KPIs that organizations focus on are lagging indicators, such as revenue, gross margin, net profit, and aged accounts receivable. These KPIs tell us what happened yesterday but don't help much in predicting and impacting tomorrow's results. Don't get me wrong—they're critically important when keeping score, but if they're all you're looking at, you'll have a difficult time driving improved results. Using only lagging indicators is a bit like driving by only looking in the rearview mirror.

· **Leading indicators**—These KPIs are both predictive of future results and, to at least some degree, are within your control. While a lagging indicator will tell you if you've reached a goal, a leading indicator will tell you if you're on track so you can take actions to increase the velocity toward your target performance. For example, your goal is to increase revenue by 20 percent (lagging indicator), some leading indicators might be the number of sales meetings you've conducted, hits on your website, number of times you've asked current clients for referrals, or your customer net promoter score.

Most companies do a great job of focusing on lagging indicators but do a poor job focusing on leading indicators. For instance, a company might be consistent about measuring employee retention but do nothing about establishing and tracking leading indicators, such as how often managers conduct one-on-one coaching with their employees.

It's vital that leaders know the difference between leading and lagging indicators and that they measure both. Each function in the functional accountability chart we discussed in Chapter 2 ("Structuring Your Leadership Team") should have two or three KPIs, and those KPIs should include both lagging and leading indicators that define success for that function.

Getting Started with a KPI Dashboard

At first, it may not be obvious what leading and lagging indicators to measure. And even when you are clear about what to measure, you may not have the right systems for measuring it.

Initially, you might have to make time-consuming manual calculations to get the numbers. Sometimes you have to design rudimentary spreadsheets that may not look pretty but give you the data you need. However, over time, those processes can be automated or streamlined—particularly when you start to enjoy the financial benefits of tracking these indicators.

Some companies start out strong and come up with two or three metrics per function and start collecting data. But then they never share it or act on it because they still aren't sure if the measurements are relevant or even accurate, so they do nothing until they figure out how to collect the right information perfectly.

That's a mistake. Don't let *perfect* be the enemy of *good*. Start collecting data right away. Some of the numbers may be inaccurate, and some may be blank because you haven't figured out how to measure it yet. That's fine. Get started and keep refining it until it becomes meaningful.

The data then needs to be compiled into a company dashboard that summarizes all of the leadership team KPIs. Regular use and review of a KPI dashboard helps your leadership team to:

1. Avoid being blindsided by something in the business that you could have seen coming

2. Focus on the right things that will drive your success

3. Spend more time solving problems and less time in verbal status updates; a good dashboard will typically reduce status updates significantly, and you can then reinvest the time saved into solving problems or executive education

A good dashboard should be:

- **Visible.** Don't hide your dashboard or hold it close to the vest. Share it widely and refer to it often. Make it visible so everyone can see exactly where the company stands. This will not only improve focus and accountability but also help generate ideas and new perspectives.

- **Simple.** The goal of the dashboard is to give you quick insights into how your company is doing. It should be straight forward without the need for a lot of explanation.

- **Actionable.** Through the use of both leading and lagging indicators, leadership team members should understand how they can impact the dashboard. If they feel the score is outside their control, they'll lose motivation and interest. Each department's leading indicators should be designed to impact the company's overarching success; otherwise, it's too easy, for example, to fault the sales department, and only the sales department, when revenues are down.

Use the Traffic Light Methodology

Dashboards can get pretty complex. People look at them and see all the numbers and their eyes glaze over. What should we be looking at? What measures really need our attention? Your marketing department has generated fifty marketing qualified leads this month. Is that good or bad?

To fix this problem, I recommend a traffic light methodology that color codes KPIs based on performance. It works as follows:

- Green—Success. KPI is achieving or beating goal.

- Yellow—In danger. KPI is below goal but not at failure level.

- Red—Failure. KPI is at or below failure level and requires immediate attention.

For instance, if you are using our earlier example of trying to increase revenue by increasing the number of sales calls, you have to decide what your goal is for that number. If your goal is to increase sales calls from thirty-five a week to fifty, any number that is fifty or higher would be color-coded green (success). Then decide what number equals failure to reach the goal. Since the goal is fifty, you wouldn't call the SWAT team if you hit forty-nine. Instead, you might define a failing grade as anything below forty. Therefore, any number of sales meetings below forty is color-coded red (failure). Anything less than the goal (fifty) but higher than the failing grade (forty) would be yellow (in danger).

Since each of the functions on your functional accountability chart—from sales and marketing to HR, IT, and finance—has two or three KPIs and are a mixture of both lagging and leading indicators, the color-coding allows you to see at a glance what part of your company is doing well and which parts need your attention. The reds become your highest priority, and the yellows become the next priority. You don't need to look at each number or listen to each department describe their leading and lagging indicators and what those numbers mean. Instead, you can zero in on the red areas and ask, "What do we need to do as a leadership team to fix this?"

Another value of having a weekly review of the KPI dashboard is that you can use it to improve the dashboard itself. Even if the dashboard is inaccurate or incomplete in areas, you can use the meeting to hold people accountable. "We keep saying this number may be inaccurate. What are we doing to make it accurate?"

In some cases, you may have to create a who-what-when (WWW) to ensure that metric becomes more accurate. We'll talk more about who-what-when later in the chapter, but for now, it describes *who* is accountable, *what* action they are accountable for, and *when* they will complete the action. While it's wise to look for ways to improve your dashboard, you shouldn't wait until everything is perfect because you'll miss opportunities in the meantime to use these KPIs in your decision-making.

Unlike company and department rocks, your KPIs don't change from quarter to quarter, but their targets may change. What was once green might one day become yellow or red as your business grows and your goals increase.

IMPLEMENT CONSISTENT PLANNING AND COMMUNICATION RHYTHMS

Most people hate meetings.

These are meetings that don't have the right agendas or any agendas at all. They're not facilitated correctly and don't happen at the right times. They don't accomplish anything, and people can't wait for them to be over so they can go back to their desk and do the real work.

But the *right* meetings lead to faster decision-making, better decision-making, more communication up and down the organization, and stronger relationships across the organization. The right meetings also provide the best platform to hold you and your team accountable for those things you're committing to every week, every month, every quarter, and every year.

When people complain about too many meetings, it's often because their organization is not implementing the right meetings with the right agendas facilitated the right way. However, when companies practice the meeting rhythm I recommend, they find many advantages, including:

- Increased productivity, as everyone is aligned on the top priorities

- Quicker decisions, as company leaders learn about challenges sooner and react to them faster

- Increased accountability throughout the organization

- Improved trust and collaboration

There are five parts to a world-class planning and communication rhythm:

1. Annual planning retreat

2. Quarterly planning and education session

3. Monthly check-in and education session

4. Weekly accountability meeting

5. Daily huddle

I'll detail each piece of the meeting rhythm below with a description as well as a sample agenda.

Conduct an Annual Planning Retreat (Two Days)

The process of aligning around priorities starts with your Breakthrough Leadership Team's annual two-day planning retreat. The retreat should be somewhere away from the office and the distractions it brings. These sessions work best with a coach or a facilitator. If you don't have a coach, the CEO typically has to lead the sessions, and that's usually not a good idea.

Why? When the leader facilitates, he or she can't also participate at the highest level, so the leadership team loses some of the insight the leader can bring. Having the CEO driving the session can also have a stifling effect on other team leaders, who may hesitate to speak up or contribute out of fear of offending the leader.

ANNUAL PLANNING RETREAT: SAMPLE AGENDA

Purpose: Review key people, strategy, execution, and cash decisions. The team will set both long-term strategy and short-term execution plans.

Duration: Two days at an off-site location

Agenda:

1. Good news/bright spots for the year
2. Pulse-check questions
3. Review results from the previous year and quarter
4. Review and confirm/adjust the company's core ideologies
5. Review and adjust the three-year plan
6. Check in on leadership team health and talent development
7. Participate in executive education to keep you sharp and keep new ideas flowing to grow the business
8. Conduct a SWOT analysis
9. Plan your next successful year and quarter
10. Plan your cascading communication

Let's break down each piece of the agenda:

1. **Good news / bright spots for the year.** I recommend leadership teams start by focusing on good news every time they meet, whether its annually, quarterly, monthly, weekly, or daily. It kicks off the meeting on a good note. It sets you on

the path of thinking more positively, and when you do that, you tend to not obsess as much over the things that went wrong. If everyone on the leadership team knows they'll be asked to share good news, they focus on finding good news, and when you focus on something, you see more of it. The goal here isn't to create a team of Pollyannas who fake positivity. Instead, the goal is to help people adopt a growth mindset, where they are focused on accomplishments and opportunities. People with a growth mindset are more positive, creative, and productive.

2. **Pulse-check questions.** After the good news, I like to pose three or four "pulse-check" questions to the leadership team. Pulse-check questions are a way to assess or even change the mood of the group. The most basic pulse-check question might be, "How are you feeling about the company right now?" But there are many others. I'll pull from my inventory of pulse-check questions (see sample questions in the callout) based on what the group is going through at the time. For example, if the leader tells me people aren't following through on their commitments, I may ask, "Looking back at the last quarter, where did you fail to make the progress you hoped for?" This provides an opening that allows team leaders to acknowledge and explain why they didn't fulfill their commitments.

SAMPLE PULSE-CHECK QUESTIONS

1. How are you feeling about the company at this time?
2. What do you believe is the number-one issue facing the company at this time?
3. What issues do we see recurring with employees?
4. What issues do we see recurring with our customers or clients?
5. What other issues must be addressed today?
6. What one conversation do we need to have that we're afraid to have?
7. In today's meeting I hope this team...
8. The concerns I have about this group and/or our tasks are...
9. What should we be most proud of as a team?
10. What should we be most proud of as a company?
11. What exciting new opportunity is on the horizon?
12. What should we stop doing?
13. What should we start doing?
14. What are our competitors doing that we need to discuss?
15. What's the most important thing we need to improve upon as a leadership team?
16. The ideal outcome for this meeting is...
17. What would you tackle next if you knew you couldn't fail?
18. What is the one thing that will change the game entirely for you? For the company?
19. What do you need to tackle that currently scares you?
20. If you could change one thing with our current strategy, what would that be?
21. What opportunity do we need to move faster on?
22. What did you fail to accomplish this quarter that you should have?

23. What is your biggest current business problem you are trying to work through or solve?
24. Looking back over the quarter, what should we have done differently?
25. What is the biggest barrier to the company moving forward right now?

3. **Review results from the previous year and quarter.** Review the financial targets, key performance indicators and accomplishments from the annual priorities from the prior year, and rocks from the previous quarter. This is a time to hold members of the leadership team accountable for their commitments. It's also a time to learn from your successes and mistakes.

4. **Review and confirm or adjust the company's core ideologies.** Review the company's core purpose, core values, and BHAG. Are these still the right core ideologies? If not, what do you need to change? If yes, how are you doing living your purpose and values? How are you progressing toward your BHAG?

5. **Review and adjust the three-year plan.** Review and update your three-year plan. What are your three-year financial targets? Are you focused on the right core customer? Do you know what will differentiate you and what market you will focus on dominating over the next three years?

6. **Check in on leadership team health and talent development.** Review the current structure and accountabilities on the leadership team. Are any changes needed to the functional accountability chart (discussed in Chapter 2)? Do you need to add any roles? Do you need to change any accountabilities? You'll also perform a "talent assessment" in which each leader assesses the people who are one level down in the organization. We'll talk more about this in the next chapter, but for now, it's how the leadership team determines its A-, B-, and C-players.

7. **Participate in executive education to keep you sharp and keep new ideas flowing to grow the business.** We'll discuss specific executive education and development ideas in the next chapter. However, this is normally a time to discuss a book the leadership team read or spend time learning a new tool or technique.

8. **Conduct a SWOT analysis.** This analysis identifies which strengths the company should leverage, which weaknesses the company should fix, which opportunities the company should pursue and which threats the company should defend itself against. The SWOT becomes a key input into the annual and quarterly plan.

9. **Plan your next successful year and quarter.** Determine your financial targets and priorities for the year as well as your financial targets, company rocks, and department

rocks for the quarter. This is the most important piece of the agenda. It's critical that all leaders understand and are aligned how success will be measured, what needs to be accomplished and who's accountable over the next year and quarter.

10. **Plan your cascading communication.** Determine what information from this planning session should and should not be communicated to the rest of the organization. It's critical to ensure clear and consistent messages about key decisions and plans.

Conduct Quarterly Planning and Education Sessions (Full-Day)

The process of aligning around priorities continues with your Breakthrough Leadership Team's full-day quarterly meeting. This meeting is typically held in the office (as opposed to the annual planning retreat, which should be held away from the office). As with the annual planning retreat, these sessions work best with a coach or a facilitator.

QUARTERLY PLANNING AND EDUCATION
SESSION: SAMPLE AGENDA

Purpose: Review last quarter's results, plan for the next quarter and participate in learning and development exercises.

Duration: One day

Agenda:

1. Good news
2. Pulse-check questions
3. Review results from the previous quarter
4. Review the company's core ideologies and three-year plan
5. Check in on leadership team health and talent development
6. Participate in executive education to keep you sharp and new ideas flowing to grow the business
7. Collaborate on a strategic opportunity
8. Plan your next successful quarter
9. Plan your cascading communication

Let's break down each piece of the agenda:

1. **Good news.** See the description from the annual planning retreat.

2. **Pulse-check questions.** See the description from the annual planning retreat.

3. **Review results from the previous quarter.** Review the quarterly financial targets and rocks as well as progress toward the annual financial targets, key performance indicators, and priorities. This is a time to hold members of the leadership team responsible for their commitments. It's also a time to learn from our successes and mistakes.

4. **Review the company's core ideologies and three-year plan.** Review core purpose, core values, BHAG, core customer, and key differentiators. Are you living and making progress on all?

5. **Check-in on leadership team health and talent development.** See description from the annual planning retreat.

6. **Participate in executive education to keep you sharp and new ideas flowing to grow the business.** See description from the annual planning retreat.

7. **Collaborate on a strategic opportunity.** Discuss any new strategic opportunities that have been identified over the last quarter. On a typical day, or in a typical, shorter meeting, there is not enough time to effectively discuss these opportunities. Leverage this time together as a leadership team to move these discussions forward.

8. **Plan your next successful quarter.** Determine your financial targets, company rocks and department rocks for the quarter.

9. **Plan your cascading communication.** See description from the annual planning retreat.

Conduct Monthly Check-In and Education Sessions (Half-Day)

The monthly check-in and education session focuses on ensuring progress toward your quarterly plan.

MONTHLY CHECK-IN AND EDUCATION SESSION: SAMPLE AGENDA

Purpose: Discuss progress on the quarterly plan, tackle key issues, and educate the leadership team on new tools and techniques.

Duration: Half day

Agenda:

1. Good news
2. Pulse check
3. Review quarterly performance to date
4. Collaborate on a strategic opportunity
5. Participate in executive education to keep you sharp and new ideas flowing to grow the business
6. Plan your cascading communication

Let's break down each piece of the agenda:

1. **Good news.** See description from the annual planning retreat.

2. **Pulse-check questions.** See description from the annual planning retreat.

3. **Review quarterly performance to date.** Review progress toward your quarterly financial targets, key performance indicators, company rocks, and department rocks. This is a time to adjust your priorities, discuss challenges and bottlenecks, and hold members of the leadership team responsible for their commitments.

4. **Collaborate on a strategic opportunity.** See description from the "Quarterly Planning and Education Session."

5. **Participate in executive education to keep you sharp and new ideas flowing to grow the business.** See description from the annual planning retreat.

6. **Plan your cascading communication.** See description from the annual planning retreat.

Conduct Weekly Accountability Meetings (Sixty Minutes)

A well-run weekly accountability meeting focuses on holding leaders accountable for progress on their company and department rocks, key performance indicators, and tasks they committed to, and is the seed from which true accountability grows. Not having this meeting or not running it well will result in poor accountability, missed goals, and frustration. This is also the easiest meeting to cancel if leaders can't make the meeting. "It's no problem, we'll just meet next week." Don't do it. Keep this ritual every week.

The method of facilitation of this meeting around accountabilities is also critical. The biggest mistake I see leaders make is allowing their leadership team members to slide by without honoring their commitments to the team. I've seen leader after leader give reasons (excuses) for not being on target with a rock or KPI, and the leader, trying to be understanding, says, "Yeah, I know you've been really busy. Let's try to get back on track soon."

This is not accountability. As a leadership team, you have determined that these rocks and KPIs are the most important things to focus on. Treat them that way. Challenge your team to honor their commitments or ask for help early and often. Challenge your team to find a way. You want results, not excuses.

WEEKLY ACCOUNTABILITY MEETING: SAMPLE AGENDA

Purpose: Discuss progress and hold team members accountable to their commitments.

Duration: One hour

Agenda:

1. Good news
2. Discuss progress on financial targets and key performance indicators
3. Discuss progress against rocks
4. Follow up on who-what-whens
5. Discuss other company and departmental updates or issues as necessary

Let's break down each piece of the agenda:

1. **Good news.** See description from the annual planning retreat.

2. **Discuss progress on financial targets and key performance indicators.** Status against company financial targets should be communicated. Status against each function's top two to three key performance indicators should be communicated. Only items in the red (failing) or in the yellow (in danger of failing) should be discussed.

3. **Discuss progress against rocks.** Each leader should be held accountable for hitting the rock milestones detailed in their plan. Only items in the red (off target) or in the yellow (off target with a chance to get back on target) need to be discussed.

4. **Follow up on who-what-whens.** See the callout below.

5. **Discuss other company and departmental issues and opportunities, as necessary.** If needed, use the remaining time in this meeting to discuss any critical issues or opportunities.

WHO-WHAT-WHENS

How many times have you been in a meeting where you thought an action was agreed to only to realize a month later that no one took the action? The team either forgot who was accountable to take the action or worse: the team forgot the whole conversation.

The who-what-when is a simple tool used during any meeting to record any actions committed to by one of the meeting participants. Whenever a new action is identified, these questions should be asked, answered, and documented:

- Who will be accountable? The answer is always and only one person.

- To the person accountable: What is the specific action you're committing to?
- To the person accountable: When are you committing to have this completed by?

Who-what-when items are typically simple, straightforward tasks that can take a day to a month. Anything more complex should be discussed as a potential rock.

Items due from the who-what-whens should be reviewed in every weekly meeting, with leaders being held accountable to the actions and dates they've committed to.

Conduct Daily Huddles (Seven to Twelve Minutes)

This short, stand-up meeting is a great way improve communication, speed decisions, and develop a much tighter, focused leadership team.

It's done in a round robin format, which means the facilitator (normally the CEO, but it doesn't need to be) quickly goes around the room and asks each leadership team member to share one after the other. For example, "Welcome to the daily huddle, let's start with good news. Joe, what's your good news?" Joe answers. "Great! Sally, what's your good news?" If this meeting lasts more than ten to twelve minutes, you're doing it wrong.

DAILY HUDDLE SAMPLE AGENDA

Purpose: Daily synchronization for the entire team, speeding decisions, and building relationships. These sessions are designed to expose opportunities and challenges but not resolve them on the spot.

Duration: Seven to twelve minutes

Agenda:

1. Good news
2. Daily metric
3. Top priority for the day
4. Where are you stuck?

Let's break down each piece of the agenda:

1. **Good news.** Each team member shares a quick piece of good news. It could be professional or personal.

2. **Daily metric.** Each team member should give an update on their most important daily key performance indicator.

3. **Top priority for the day.** Each team member shares the most important thing they plan to work on that day.

4. **Where are you stuck?** Each team member shares some-

thing that's challenging them at the moment. This is NOT the time to solve the problem. The facilitator might ask, "Is there someone here that can help you with that?" but that's as far as it goes. If you try to solve problems in a daily huddle, these meetings will last thirty minutes, and people will stop attending.

SOME FINAL THOUGHTS ON DISCIPLINED EXECUTION

Here are some additional tips that will help ensure disciplined execution that drives real results:

- **In your annual planning, don't expect to craft the perfect plan.** Get the strategic plan 70 to 80 percent accurate, and then get the right people to execute the hell out of that imperfect plan. You will then learn and adjust—constantly.

- **Don't be paralyzed by difficult decisions.** In fact, wrong decisions are often better than making no decision at all. At the very least, a wrong decision teaches you an important lesson and may reveal the correct route. Doing nothing gets you nowhere. Have a bias toward action.

- **It's all about the quarterly plan.** The most important part of your strategic plan is your quarterly plan; that's where the real work happens. Your quarterly plans create focus and urgency. Quarterly rocks don't allow room for procrastination. All of the longer-term planning work you do is for the purpose of deciding what needs to be accomplished in the next ninety days.

- **Get a coach.** I realize this sounds self-serving, but I wouldn't say it if it weren't true. A good coach can help create an environment for accountability. It takes time to build these habits and disciplines, and it's easy to fall off track. A coach will help keep you on track. A good coach also helps your company's leaders—particularly the CEO—transition from the whirlwind of daily business work to the more productive role as a visionary.

As your leadership team gets comfortable with your planning process and communication rhythms, allow those practices to cascade down through your organization. Individual departments and teams can and should use these tools, and members of your leadership team should be prepared to coach their people on the best practices for using the tools we discuss in this chapter.

The three disciplines of execution—aligning around priorities, measuring what matters, and implementing a consistent planning and communication rhythm—enable you to quickly focus on the most important actions for your company.

They allow you to work *on* the business and not just work *in* the business.

CHAPTER 6

DEVELOPING AND IMPROVING YOUR TEAM

I recently started working with the leadership team for a company where the CEO is a lot like me: we're both avid readers. I probably read about a book a week, and the CEO shares my belief that reading is crucial to your personal growth. Reading introduces you to new ideas and approaches.

The CEO and I wanted his leadership team to read too. We felt his leadership team needed to be learning more if it was going to meet its aggressive growth targets. The CEO and I suggested his leadership team read one book a quarter and share the ideas they gleaned. Neither of us thought this would be difficult for his leaders to accomplish, and we thought they would enjoy it.

But we got some pushback.

"I don't have time for that," said one of his department heads. "You don't understand my life. I start work at eight in the morning, and I'm here till seven. I get home at eight, and I'd like to spend a little bit of time with my family."

I offered a few ideas that might help him. You have a long commute, I said. Why not listen to audiobooks or podcasts in the car? What about finding time in the evening after everyone's gone to bed to read for forty-five minutes? Were there some duties that he could delegate so he didn't have to stay so late? I tried to sound encouraging and empathetic.

Nothing worked.

"Listen," he said. "When I've had a stressful day, I want to just go home and breathe."

I switched to a more direct message.

"You may not like what I'm about to say, but if you're going to be a strong member of this leadership team, you need to be learning. You need to be reading. You're not an accounts-payable clerk who's being told what to do every day. You're a leader. You need to figure out how to find the time."

The CEO was happy to hear this because he agrees with me that if you're not learning and growing, you are dying. For a company, a leadership team, or an individual, there are always new things to learn and new ways to get better. If you believe that you know all you need to know and that all you need to do now is execute, you're gravely mistaken. The world around you, including your competition, is continually changing, expanding, and getting more complex. If you remain static, you'll be left behind. When you stop trying to improve, your skills and knowledge start to calcify. Boredom sets in and your motivation wanes. Your passion fades. Your ability to execute declines.

You don't want to be that person. That kind of person has a dampening effect on the rest of the team, making everyone, including the CEO, work harder and enjoy their work less.

In fact, one of the factors I consider when deciding whether to take on a new client is whether the CEO is a lifelong learner. As I've already mentioned, I'm an avid reader. If I go thirty minutes without recommending a book, call 9-1-1 because I'm probably having a stroke. When I'm chatting for the first time with a prospective client, I'll ask the CEO about the last book that really had an impact on how he or she is leading their team. If I hear something like, "Books? Who has time for reading? I haven't read a book in a year," that's a warning sign that this client may not be ready for coaching.

I hope this chapter convinces you that, as a member or leader of an executive team, you must continue developing and improving. Sometimes that means each person on the team improves as an individual. Sometimes that means the whole team is working together to improve their relationships, collaboration, and communication. And sometimes it means pruning the team to allow those B- and C-players on the leadership team who don't challenge themselves to find other opportunities. You need people who are willing to scale up as your company scales up. CEOs can help those who want it, but people are accountable for their own growth.

Leaders should ask themselves every quarter, *What am I going to do in the next ninety-days to grow my team?* This isn't so they can plan group training, because each leader on that team may need a different type of training. Instead, it's an overarching question that helps leaders analyze their team's strengths and weaknesses, address gaps in the team's skills and knowledge, and take specific steps to fill those gaps. Each leader also needs to ask that question of themselves: *Where do I need to perform better this quarter?*

WARNING SIGNS

Leadership teams that don't purposefully learn and grow together run into a number of problems: key employees leave, company revenue stagnates, and progress toward quarterly goals stalls. Those are just some of the overarching results, but there are other signs that your leadership team isn't scaling with your business. Here are a few of the more crucial ones.

LEADERS DON'T COMPLETE THEIR ROCKS

Your quarterly planning process determines what's most important for the next ninety days and who's accountable for accomplishing that goal. What you start to see when your leaders aren't growing with your company is that they struggle to complete those rocks in time because they can't overcome the big obstacles they face. They're not hitting their key performance indicators—particularly the leading indicators—and this holds the rest of the team back.

LEADERS ARE HESITANT TO CHALLENGE THEMSELVES

The rocks these leaders propose aren't challenging or aggressive enough to have real impact on the business. You also start to see that your leaders who aren't growing with the company tend to retreat to the dark corners of the conference room; when the conversations turn to ambitious goals, they grow silent and don't participate. They add less value to the conversation since they haven't professionally grown and don't have the knowledge or ambition to think strategically or weigh in with creative and relevant ideas.

PEOPLE ARE OVERWHELMED

When your company's leaders aren't improving their own skills at the rate the business needs to accomplish its goals, they find themselves treading water or drowning, unable to perform at the level the company needs them to. Your head of operations may have been outstanding when you were a $10 million company, but now that you're a $50 million company, that person might have three different warehouses, more products and services, and a three-year plan to double the operations. It's more than they can handle. They haven't grown sufficiently to manage these new challenges.

As a result, they often retreat to their departmental silos and stop thinking of the leadership team as their #1 team. If they are in operations, they pay scant attention to what's happening in marketing. As a leadership team, you start losing that sense of how all the departments within your business should work together.

COMPANY GROWTH STAGNATES

If your leadership team includes B- and C-players that aren't improving, your company's revenue and growth will stagnate or start shrinking. You'll start to miss your quarterly revenue and profitability targets, and you may lose valuable employees as a result. These departing employees will tell you they're leaving for more money or a better opportunity, but the real reason is that they can see the leadership of the company has stagnated. The employees don't feel challenged to grow, and they sense the need to go elsewhere if they want to make that next jump in their career.

THE CEO TAKES ON TOO MUCH

When there are B- and C-players on the leadership team who aren't interested in learning and improving, CEOs may see their leadership team's work not getting done, resulting in a greater majority of the challenging work falling to the CEO. This can have a detrimental effect on the CEO's own growth and development. When they feel like they have to do everyone's job for them, CEOs stop looking for their own opportunities to grow, and that also hurts the company. The CEO becomes a poor model for the rest of the company; their disregard for self-improvement trickles down. Bottom line: if a CEO doesn't grow and improve, the company will not grow and improve.

A-PLAYERS LEAVE THE LEADERSHIP TEAM

When a company doesn't emphasize the growth and improvement of their leaders, you risk losing the A-players on your leadership team and below. A-players want to be part of a great team, and when they are not being challenged to be their best, or others around them are not challenging themselves to be their best, one of two things can happen.

First, an A-player becomes a B-player and continues working for you, although in a diminished and uninspired way. Or the A-player leaves the company. They will tell you they're leaving "for a better opportunity," but the truth is they leave because they weren't being challenged to grow.

DEVELOPING AND IMPROVING YOUR TEAM: AN ACTION PLAN FOR LEARNING AND GROWING

To have a vibrant, growing business, you must focus on four layers of development:

1. **Leadership team development**—As a team, learning new tools and techniques improves leadership team function and health. Examples can include doing team-building activities, reading books together, attending training sessions, or going to conferences.

2. **Professional self-development**—This is when individuals on the team gain new skills, knowledge, and experience. Examples can include reading books and attending training sessions or conferences to learn new interpersonal or technical skills.

3. **Personal self-development**—This is when individuals on the team focus on improving mind, body, and spirit. Examples can include exercise, meditation, starting a new hobby, and learning, especially when it has nothing to do with work.

4. **Direct reports development**—As a leader, you need to ensure your direct reports are learning and growing as well. (If you're the CEO, your direct reports are the leadership team, so this point is somewhat redundant with #1 on this list). Examples can include team-building, reading books,

and attending training or conferences to learn new interpersonal or technical skills.

This is not to say one layer is more important than the others or that you need to complete one level before you move on to the next. Each layer needs your attention. You should be working on your growth as an individual at the same time that you are working on growth with your teams. It also helps to go back from time to time and revisit each layer and assess whether you need to do more work in that area.

Below are several ways to get you started. Pick two or three to start with and then sprinkle in some other approaches from time to time to keep things fresh.

READ, READ, READ

The best way for a team to learn and grow together is to read, whether it's books, industry publications, white papers, or magazine articles. Continuous learning can be as simple and easy as having everyone on the team read a book, discuss it, and find ideas from those books that the team can inject into its DNA. I recommend teams read a book a quarter.

One way to cull the best ideas is to have everyone on the team jot down on a Post-it Note their top three ideas for action from the material the group has just read. Put those Post-its on a flip chart and group similar ones together. After you discuss the ideas, vote on your top three to five and ask for volunteers to be accountable for incorporating the idea into the company culture. If no one volunteers to do it, that tells you that the idea isn't important enough to inject into your DNA.

When people are eager to adopt an idea, execute with discipline and determine who is going to be accountable for ensuring it happens. What specifically are they going to do and what's the deadline? If you don't take it seriously and create a who-what-when (discussed in Chapter 5), the idea will never be adopted.

THE RIGHT BOOK AT THE RIGHT TIME

When deciding on what books to read, leadership teams should consider what challenges their company is facing and find books that address those challenges.

I worked with one company where the financial literacy of the leadership team was low. When I used language from the P&L, balance sheet, or cash-flow statement, I could see some people were lost. CEOs and leaders are often too embarrassed to admit they don't understand financial matters, so I had them read *The Accounting Game: Lessons from a Lemonade Stand* by Darrell Mullis and Judith Orloff.

Figure 17 lists some other sample leadership team situations and the books I recommend for each.

Fig. 17

Situation	Recommended Book
Lack of Trust	*The Five Dysfunctions of a Team* by Pat Lencioni
Need for better coaching and mentoring skills	*Multipliers* by Liz Wiseman *The Coaching Habit* by Michael Bungay Stanier
Too many hiring mistakes	*Who: The A Method for Hiring* by Geoffrey Smart *Hiring for Attitude* by Mark Murphy
Team lacks strategic thinking capabilities	*Good to Great* by Jim Collins *The 3HAG Way* by Shannon Susko
Morale or culture issues on the team	*The Culture Code* by Daniel Coyle *The Power of Moments* by Chip and Dan Heath
Lack of accountability	*Measure What Matters* by John Doerr *The Five Dysfunctions of a Team* by Pat Lencioni

FIND AND LEVERAGE YOUR TEAM'S NATURAL TALENTS

A fundamental part of growing professionally and personally is understanding your natural talents. As a leader, you play a central role in discovering your own talents as well as others on the leadership team and your direct reports. As we discussed in Chapter 1 ("Self-Leadership"), all members of the leadership team should take a strengths assessment—I recommend StrengthsFinder 2.0—and share the results with the rest of the team.

I use a powerful process with my leadership teams (and their teams) to help them better understand the natural talents on their team and coach each other on how to leverage those talents. Here's the process:

As Individuals

1. Read *StrengthsFinder 2.0* by Tom Rath.

2. Take the Strengthsfinder 2.0 Assessment to identify your top strengths.

3. For each strength, answer the following questions:

   A. What will you do to turn this talent into a strength (or stronger strength)? How will you increase knowledge, skills, and practice?

   B. How will you better leverage this talent or strength every day? How are you committed to give these gifts to the world?

As a Team

1. Have each team member share and discuss their top strength as well as the answer to the questions in #3 of the previous list.

2. After each team member has shared the information on

their top strength, have the team pair up and take turns coaching each other on additional ways to improve and leverage the strength.

3. Repeat this process for everyone's top five strengths.

4. Discuss, as a team, any important talents that don't exist on the leadership team. How is it impacting your team's performance? What can you do to compensate for this lack of talent?

FOCUS ON PERSONAL DEVELOPMENT

It's easy to just focus on professional development. After all, we're talking about work, aren't we? I have found that personal development is at least as important as professional development. If we are better people, we'll become better leaders and team members. If we're better outside of work, we'll be better at work.

Leaders and their companies must make sure they are giving the leadership team personal education and development opportunities as well. I introduce my clients to such resources as Shawn Achor's book *The Happiness Advantage*, which subscribes to the premise that success doesn't necessarily bring happiness, but that happiness often leads to success.

As part of that training, the team members and I brainstorm

the different ways people around the table primed themselves for the beginning of the day. Some meditated or prayed to start the day, while others worked out or reflected on the things for which they're grateful.

We also discussed how to manage emotional disruptions during the day. What do you do to get your head back on straight? Some people went out for a walk or took a break to exercise. Some listened to their favorite songs. Some called their spouse or a friend and talked it out.

Your company can help employees develop strong tactics for personal development and physical and emotional health. Bring in a meditation instructor. Offer free gym memberships or mass-transit passes so your workers don't have to deal with a stressful commute. When ordering in food, skip the pepperoni pizza in favor of something healthier. Encourage walking. I know of one government agency in Colorado that hands out pedometers to employees and pays them up to $300 a month if they average 10,000 steps a day. I know another company that has a quarterly competition to see who can lose the highest percentage of body fat.

Some leaders have the philosophy that because their employees helped them achieve a dream, the company has an obligation to return the favor.

For example, one of my clients read a book by Matthew Kelly

called *The Dream Manager.* They then brought in one of his consultants to develop a program in their company that helped employees realize their dreams. This didn't mean employees who dreamed of living in a European mansion got a chateau in France. Instead, consultants came in and met staff to discuss their dreams and helped them map out a path to realizing them. If the employee is living in a tiny apartment but dreams of buying a house, the consultant will work with them on a budget and a spending plan that gets that person closer to their dream.

If any of this sounds too expensive or time-consuming for your company, keep in mind that programs that improve staff mental and physical health have a direct impact on your bottom line. Healthy people with strong self-awareness and emotional control are more productive, focused, and engaged.

LEARN WITHIN THE NORMAL PLANNING AND COMMUNICATION RHYTHM

Not everything you do to develop and improve your team involves a special program involving yoga instructors or dream managers. Some are as simple as watching an eighteen-minute TED Talk during your quarterly meeting and then discussing any ideas your leadership team can adopt.

If it's not a TED Talk, it could be a simple reflection exercise. What did we learn from our mistakes last quarter? What did we learn from our success? Have each leader jot down three lessons they've gleaned from the last three months on Post-it Notes and then discuss these as a group. You can pick the best ones, and then take a specific action to ensure your new understanding becomes a part of your DNA. Do a who-what-when. If you don't have a specific action, you'll only have to learn the lesson all over again.

It could also be learning a new tool or technique as a team. I've incorporated education on how to be a better coach, how to have difficult conversations, how to read a P&L statement, and others into the normal monthly and quarterly meeting rhythms I facilitate with my clients.

CONDUCT ONE-ON-ONE COACHING SESSIONS

At least once every two weeks (ideally every week), the CEO and each member of the leadership team should meet with their direct reports to coach them.

Most companies screw this up and make the one-on-one an accountability session. "Did you get this done? How are we doing on this thing?"

That's not what the one-on-one is about. Save the accountability questions for the weekly meeting. The one-on-one is about coaching and helping, and the discussion should be driven by the direct report, who should come to the meeting with something they want to talk about. For example, they might ask:

- How do I remove this obstacle that I'm facing?

- I'm having trouble with this particular department. How should I handle it?

- I'd like to do a better job at X and I need some help. What do you suggest?

- I'd like to take the next step in my career and learn how to do X, Y, and Z. Is there a way you can help me do that?

One of the most important skills a leader needs to learn is how to be a coach. The two most important skills of a great coach are (1) helping the person being coached identify the real problem, and (2) helping the person being coached decide on their right action. Let's briefly discuss both.

1. **Helping the person being coached identify the real problem.** One of the biggest mistakes a coach can make is to coach someone on the wrong problem. For example, one of your direct reports tells you the website project is running late, and they're having a hard time working with the graphic design team. You might jump right in and give them advice on how to better manage a large project. Or you might give them a fifteen-minute dissertation on how to work with difficult people. You're assuming you know what the real problem is. But you typically don't. Michael Bungay Stanier, in *The Coaching Habit,* recommends a very simple

question he calls "the focus question" to help cut through the fog to get to the real issue. Before jumping in to solve the problem, simply ask, "What's the real challenge here for you?" By asking that question, you may find out the real challenge is that your direct report feels like they're letting the team down and it's stressing them out. They don't need advice on how to manage the project or deal with the graphic design team. They just need help figuring out good ways to deal with the stress.

2. **Helping the person being coached decide on their right action.** Coaching is not about giving advice. It's about asking questions to help people come up with the right action for them, which might be different than the action you would take if you were in their shoes. That's one of the problems with giving advice: we all have different needs, wants, talents, and styles, so the right actions may be very different from person to person. Another problem with giving advice is we're not teaching people how to solve the problem themselves. We're teaching them to come to us so we can solve the problem for them. The key for a great coach is to ask the right questions that model how the person being coached could think about it and coach themselves through it the next time. Again, I'll recommend *The Coaching Habit* as a great source to learn the right questions.

These one-on-one sessions should last thirty to forty-five minutes, and the direct report being coached by the leader should be having similar sessions with their direct reports. Meanwhile, the leader should use an outside coach who can challenge them in ways their leadership team won't.

LEARN AND TEACH

In addition to the learning that leadership team members do together, team members can seek out individual training that they then bring back to the group as a whole. This approach allows each team member to decide what they need to learn—either to be a better team member or to be a better leader for their departments and direct reports—and then get that training.

This training can be function-specific. For example, a chief financial officer may need to learn more about cash flow optimization. The head of operations may need to learn more about logistics software. The training could be as simple as reading a book, listening to a podcast, doing some research on the web, or attending a conference.

When the training is over, the team members bring back the knowledge to the full leadership group. They might give a thirty-minute presentation to the group during its next quarterly meeting. Knowing that they'll be asked to present on this new knowledge encourages the leaders to analyze the material and determine how it applies to the team's work. You learn better when you know you have to teach the topic to someone else.

THE BENEFITS OF LEARNING

Teams that learn together are much less likely to either fall into a rut or think they've got everything figured out. Continual learning makes them question what they're doing and prompts them to say, "Wait a minute. There's got to be another way." When you're learning and growing, you realize there's a lot you don't know, and that makes you hungry for even more knowledge.

Here are other benefits of a team learning together:

- The questions team members ask are more creative and challenging.

- The ability of each team member to help another team member skyrockets.

- When each team member learns on their own, it makes the entire team smarter.

- The team's and the company's thinking are continually injected with fresh ideas, including leading-edge ideas culled from other industries.

- The team's emphasis on learning cascades down through the organization, making everyone more inquisitive and bringing an even greater wealth of knowledge to the company.

- Your A-players stay with you because they have an opportunity to learn and grow and because they are working with people with similar sensibilities.

Teams that learn and grow together bring returns to your company the same way compounding interest increases your savings. If you're getting 1 percent better every day, after a year, you're not 365 percent better but something on the order of a million times better. This is not about doing one training a year that makes a few people 10 percent better. It's about training and learning a little bit every day—acquiring skill and knowledge that gets compounded so that by the end of the year, you don't resemble the company you were a year before.

TRACK YOUR LEARNING AND DEVELOPMENT

To support the planning and tracking of your leadership team learning and development, I recommend the accompanying tool (Figure 18) to ensure focus on both professional and personal development for you as an individual, for the leadership team, and for your direct reports. You can use this to plan at the beginning of the year and revise it each quarter as you complete development activities and your needs as an individual and team continue to change.

Fig. 18

Month	Individual		Leadership Team		Direct Reports	
	Personal	Professional	Personal	Professional	Personal	Professional
January						
February						
March						
April						
May						
June						
July						
August						
September						
October						
November						
December						

DEVELOPING AND IMPROVING YOUR TEAM: AN ACTION PLAN FOR ASSESSING YOUR TALENT

The most important job of a leader is to surround yourself with the right talent. For that reason, I advocate companies do a quarterly talent assessment, both at the leadership team level and at the next level down—the people who report directly to the leaders on the leadership team.

One of the biggest mistakes companies make is evaluating

people solely on productivity. If a salesperson brings in sacksful of cash, they're an A-player. If someone in accounting is a whiz at database queries to analyze expense accounts, they're an A-player. The problem with that is that it disregards the impact those people are having on your company culture. Are they living your core values? How are they impacting the productivity and morale of those around them?

The quarterly process I use with my clients allows you to identify and discuss your:

1. **A-Players**—These are your superstars. They are not only the strongest members of your organization, but they are in the top 10 percent in their field. They are talented and skilled, but they also embody your company's core values and serve as a model for the rest of the company. These are the people you, as a leader in the company, want to spend the most time with. You want to coach and challenge them, give them more responsibility and money, promote them, recognize them, and understand their career goals so that you can help them achieve those goals. These are the people you want to keep, so you look for ways to make sure they never want to leave.

2. **B-players**—These are good, solid performers, but they aren't superstars—yet. You want to coach and mentor your best B-players with the goal of converting them to A-players or at least making them strong B-players. Sometimes this

means you change their role to leverage their strengths with the aim of turning them into A-players.

3. **C-players**—These are the people who are hurting your organization. They either don't embrace your company's core values, and/or their productivity is so low that it's having a major negative impact on the team. Most importantly, these C-players threaten your greatest asset: your A-players. A-players become frustrated with team members that hold them or the company back through toxic behavior or low productivity. Before that happens, identify your C-players and coach them to some level of acceptable performance or cut the cord and let them go work for the competition.

This process is not a replacement for a formal performance review process you may have in place. This is a process to drive conversation and debate about the level of talent in the organization. It helps answer the following questions:

- Do we have the right talent in the organization to drive us to meet our short- and long-term goals?

- Who are the superstars we need to recognize, reward, and challenge?

- Who are our potential superstars, and how do we get them to the next level?

- Which team members are holding us back, and are they coachable?

CONDUCT A QUARTERLY TALENT ASSESSMENT

Here's the process I recommend you follow each quarter (in the "Quarterly Planning and Education Session," see Chapter 5 for the full agenda for this meeting):

1. **List the names of all the people you are assessing on the talent assessment details form** (Figure 19). If you are the VP of Operations and you have five direct reports, you would list each one here. (Note: the CEO is not evaluating members of the leadership team in this meeting. Those assessments are made privately by the CEO in consultation with the CEO's business coach.)

Fig. 19

Team Member Initials	Core Value Score (0-10)	Productivity Score (0-10)	Action Plan

2. **Give each person a core values score and a productivity score on a scale of zero to ten.** Use whole numbers when scoring. No one gets a 7.5; round up or down. Don't make scoring into a giant math problem. Keep things simple. If they are a living, breathing example of the core values every day, they're probably a 9 or a 10. If they consistently and repeatedly break one or more core values, their score will go down appropriately. If they are consistently completing their rocks and hitting their KPIs, their productivity score will probably be very high. If they are missing goals consistently...you get the idea.

3. **Decide, as a company, how you are defining A-, B-, and C-players.** Draw a talent assessment chart (see Figure 20) on a flip chart to be ready for the next step. As a team, agree on what numbers will replace the boxed question marks on the first page of the form. These numbers will determine where people fall on the talent assessment (A, B, C or Toxic C).

Fig. 20

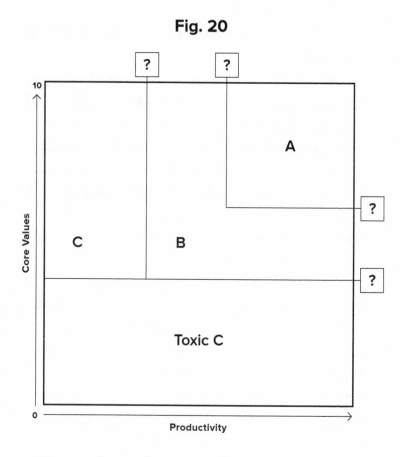

Here are the numbers I strongly recommend:

- **A-Players**—I recommend putting an 8.5 in the boxes next to the horizontal and vertical lines around the A square. That means that in order to be an A-player, you must score nine or higher in both core values and productivity. Notice I always end my numbers with .5, as this forces people into the categories (A, B, C, or Toxic-C) without anyone being on the line.

- **Toxic C-Players**—Examine the bottom square labeled 'Toxic C." Notice how it stretches across the bottom of the chart. This means that no matter how productive you are, if you're not embracing the company's core values, you're toxic. The question for the company is, How low does a core value score have to be to make someone toxic? That's the box on the right, below the box you just filled in for A-Players. I recommend using 7.5 (again, use a fraction so no one falls on the line). That means anyone who scores seven or below in core values is determined to be toxic to your organization. I know that sounds harsh, but remember, your core values are nonnegotiable behaviors. Scoring a 7 out of 10 on nonnegotiable behaviors should be unacceptable.

- **C-Players**—The next piece of the puzzle is the question box in the upper left. This measures another type of C-player. These are folks who may be embodying your core values, but their productivity is so low that they are hurting the company. They aren't toxic. In fact, they may be wonderful people who fit in well, but they are not productive. I recommend putting a 6.5 in that question box (again, use a fraction so no one falls on the line). That means anyone that scores a 6 or below in productivity is determined to be a C-player. If they are also below a 7.5 in core values, they would be Toxic C.

- **B-players**—We don't need to fill in any more boxed

question marks here. These are your solid to mediocre folks who score high enough in core values and productivity to not be C- or Toxic C-Players, but don't score high enough to be A-players.

4. **Have each member of the leadership team write the initials for each person on a small Post-it Note along with their scores (core values first, productivity second).** If you were evaluating Mike Goldman, you would write "MG 8, 9."

5. **Have each leader, one at a time, share their scores** with the others so the leadership team knows the talent everyone else has on their departmental team. For instance, the head of operations might say, "I gave Joe Bennett, the director of warehousing, an eight in core values and an eight in productivity. Joe is a B-player." Then the head of operations puts the Post-it with "JB 8, 8" on the talent assessment chart. Then she does the same for all of her other direct reports.

6. **The other leaders support or challenge each other's scores as needed.** Leadership team members may have seen things in people that their fellow leaders haven't. "Wait a minute. How can you give Bob a ten for core values? I saw him screaming at somebody out in the hallway yesterday." You can't discuss every person because you'll be there all day, but this is the right time to bring up conflicting assessments and questions.

7. **Once all the scores are on the flip chart, do a quick calculation to determine what percentage of people are A, B, C, or Toxic C.** Then I ask, "What do we think of our talent this quarter?" The team may be thrilled. Seventy percent of their people might be superstars, and they don't have any Toxic Cs. On the other hand, they may have a bunch of Toxic Cs and only one or two A-players. Then they might be thinking, *We've got a big problem here.*

8. **Regardless of how the chart shapes up, the team must ask itself, "What did we do to cause this result?"** If they have 70 percent superstars, this might be a sign that their hiring and coaching practices are strong. However, if their ranks are shot through with C-players, they may want to talk about hiring better or doing more effective coaching.

9. **Focus on A-players.** It may seem counterintuitive to focus first on A-players. Shouldn't we focus first on training and mentoring the B- and C-players? The answer is no. A-players have the greatest potential for growth, the most potential to help your company skyrocket to the moon, the most potential to one day take a seat at the leadership table, and the most potential to get job offers somewhere else. The worst thing you can do for an A-player is say, "Thank God for Susan. She's a superstar, so I can just leave her alone and go focus on my B- and C-players." You should be spending most of your time with your A-players. They are what will make you great. So I'll ask, "What kinds of things should

we be doing with these folks?" When I do that, I'll get comments like:

A. Let's re-recruit them.

B. Let's take steps to ensure they want to stay with us.

C. Let's recognize their work publicly and privately.

D. Let's challenge them and give them harder work so they remain challenged.

E. Let's give them more training.

F. Let's do a better job of leveraging their strengths.

G. Let's coach and mentor them more.

H. Let's promote them.

10. **While this discussion is taking place, the leaders jot down on the second page of the form their action plan for those A-players that directly report to them.** The leaders should have a different action plan for each A-player. One A-player may be overdue for a promotion, while another may only need a pat on the back. Each quarter, these leaders should have an action plan to mentor, coach, challenge, or reward these A-players.

11. **Create action plans for your B-players.** Your goal is to coach B-players to become A-players. There are two possibilities for turning a B-player into an A-player. First, you can coach them to improve productivity and/or core values in the current role. Second, you can change their role to better leverage their strengths. Doing this can raise their productivity (by focusing on their natural talents) and their core values (they might do a better job of living the values if they're focused on what they love doing).

12. **Ask yourself a critical question about each of your C- and Toxic C-players:** Are you going to coach or cut the cord? Everyone deserves a chance to succeed. Everyone deserves coaching if they're not meeting the requirements of the job. However, I've seen too many companies hold on to C- and Toxic C-players for one to two years, hoping and praying that things will improve. That's not fair to your company and not fair to the low-performing team member. Everyone can be an A-player somewhere. If they can't do it within your organization, you need to set them free to do it somewhere else.

   For my clients, if a leader decides they are going to coach, they have ninety days—until the next quarterly meeting— to get performance up into at least the B-player level. If the improvement doesn't happen, but you still want to give them more coaching, guess what? *You* may be the C-player.

CUT THE CORD

In my interviews with CEOs, 90 percent of them said their biggest mistake was holding on to the wrong people too long. The quarterly talent assessment forces leaders and CEOs to have the difficult discussions with their team members about their behavior, performance, or uncertain future with the organization. Without this talent assessment, problems fester. Conducting the assessment with the rest of the leadership team holds everyone accountable because no leader wants to show up every quarter and admit their C-players continue to be C-players or that they are not increasing the number of A-players on their team. Peer pressure forces action.

When it comes to making the hard decisions about C or Toxic-C players, here are some of the reasons (excuses) leaders use to defend inaction:

- **We owe this person our loyalty.** Sometimes these problems linger out of misplaced loyalty. Leaders don't want to cut the cord with an employee because they have been with the company for fifteen years and the leader feels loyal to them. When I hear that, I ask these leaders, "Are you more loyal to this one person than you are to the rest of the organization? This one person is hurting the other ninety-nine employees; are they less important than this one person?"

- **We'll be short-staffed.** Many leaders put off cutting the cord because they feel it will leave them short-handed. This is the C-player trap. There's no sense of urgency to find somebody else if the position is still filled. And while you're procrastinating and avoiding the difficult conversation, the C-player continues to hurt your organization. Many leaders don't realize that when you cut the cord on a C-player, everyone else's productivity goes up. Remember, too, that the productivity of one superstar typically equals that of three mediocre performers (as we discussed in Chapter 2). You can remove three C-players, hire one A-player, and have a happier, more productive company.

- **We can do more coaching.** When I ask teams, "Are they coachable, or should we cut the cord?" many leaders hem and haw.

"I'm not God," they'll say. "I'm not all-knowing. How do I know if they're coachable?"

I understand their hesitation. It's a big decision to cut the cord. Firing someone—even someone who has been holding you back and making your team miserable for two years—is not easy to do. This is someone's life. It's not just a Post-it Note stuck on a flip chart. But you must be honest: you *do* know if they are coachable. Is it possible there is one more coaching strategy that you haven't tried yet? Maybe. But are you willing to hold your organization hostage while you figure that out?

- **A-players cost too much.** Sometimes when I'm doing this exercise with a leadership team, someone will raise a hand and say, "Do we *really* want all A-players? If everyone's an A player, everyone's going to want more money and a promotion! We can't promote everyone." I typically have two responses:

  - **Not all A-players want a promotion.** For example, you can have an accounts payable clerk who is outstanding and has done incredible work for the last thirty years. But they have no interest in moving up or becoming a CFO. They love what they do, and they want to keep doing it.

  - **If you have all A-players, you can afford to pay them more.** I ask my clients to trust me on this: if you had all A-players, your company will be growing fast enough and profitably enough to give everyone promotions and more money. Are you going to purposely limit your organization's growth just so you don't have to give top performers raises? I don't think so.

If your team starts to use these excuses, have your leaders try to see cutting the cord in a more positive light. In addition to releasing your company from the bondage of C-players, you may be helping the C-player out when you let them go. Remember, C-players aren't bad people; they're just a bad fit for your organization. Everyone can be an A-player somewhere doing something, so when you cut the cord with a C-player, you are freeing them up to be an A-player somewhere else.

And let's be brutally honest here: most of these reasons (excuses) are code for "I'm really uncomfortable having difficult conversations, so I'd rather keep delaying things." Not only does this cause leaders indecision about cutting the cord, it also causes them to procrastinate about doing real coaching with these individuals. And that's just unfair to everyone.

It's time to confront the problem. Keeping them on the team performing at a C level is a bad situation for all involved. Set them free to realize their potential and to feel fulfilled in a job that's a better fit for who they are.

CHAPTER 7

CALL TO ACTION

You've just finished reading this book, and your head is swimming with ideas. You're probably wondering, *Where do I begin?*

I suggest you start by measuring where you are in your journey toward becoming a Breakthrough Leadership Team, then prioritize opportunities for improvement, take action, learn from those actions, and repeat the process again. You'll make both revolutionary and evolutionary progress along the way.

MEASURING WHERE YOU ARE ON THE JOURNEY TO BECOME A BREAKTHROUGH LEADERSHIP TEAM

We strive to become a Breakthrough Leadership Team so we can create a great company. So let's quickly review the three characteristics of a great company. As a review, they are:

- Sustained top- and bottom-line growth

- A place where employees can feel fulfilled and grow

- A company that adds value to society

All of these characteristics are important to a healthy, growing company. Even if your company is making money, you can't remain profitable for long if you aren't creating the right environment for your employees or if you're not having the right impact on society.

Just as you can measure top- and bottom-line growth, you can also measure the other two qualities of a great company.

For instance, if you want to know if your company is a place where people love to work and feel fulfilled by that work, consider giving your employees an employee net promoter survey. Many companies are using net promoter scores to better serve their customers, but you can also use them to better serve your employees.

An employee net promoter score, which we discussed in Chapter 4 ("Defining the Right Culture"), asks two basic questions:

- How likely are you to recommend someone work for this company?

- What can we do to improve this score?

The first question is a numerical rating that works this way:

respondents rate the company on a scale of 0 (don't work here even if your life depended on it) to 10 (it's great!). People who score you a 9 or 10 are considered promoters, and those who rate you a 0 to 6 are detractors. You get your net promoter score by subtracting the percent of promoters from your percent detractors (7s and 8s are considered neutral and are not counted). Your final score will fall somewhere between –100 percent to +100 percent.

Under this scoring rubric, you can't think of your score the way you would your grade on a test. For example, 70 percent is a mediocre test score—it's just barely a C grade—but on an employee net promotor survey, it's a fantastic score.

The greatest value in the survey, though, is in the written responses to the second question. (What can we do to improve this score?) Here is where you can drill down and uncover why you scored what you did. This is where people can complain about poor communication, a lack of direction, or problems with C-players who hang around year after year, making everyone miserable.

There are other ways to assess where you stand on being a good place to work. For example:

- **What's your employee retention?** If 30 percent of your workforce leaves every year, you are not providing a growth-focused, fulfilling environment.

- **Is your percentage of A-players rising?** In Chapter 6 ("Developing and Improving Your Team"), we described the quarterly talent assessment exercise and how you can see what proportion of your workforce is A-, B-, C- and Toxic C-players. Are those numbers getting any better?

- **Have you been able to promote really good people?** This measurement is tied both to top- and bottom-line growth and the existence of A-players on your team.

The third quality of a great company—the value you bring to society—is a little harder to measure objectively, but there are ways to do it. A good customer net promoter score would suggest that customers value your contribution to their quality of life. Customer retention numbers might also provide insights.

While it may be harder to measure, this characteristic is crucial for most companies. That's because this quality matters tremendously to both team members and clients. When I first started out as a consultant for a large firm, I was intently focused on one thing: making partner. Making partner meant more money, status, and fulfillment.

In contrast, today's professionals in their twenties and thirties are not working just so they can drive a BMW. They care about the world, and they want their work to address the issues they care about, whether it's global warming, gun control, poverty, income imbalance, equal pay for equal work, natural resources, violence, or racism. They want to feel like they're having an impact.

Often when I'm meeting with a client for the first time and I bring up these three qualities, someone at the table smirks. "This sounds nice," they say, "but we all know we're here to make money."

My response is, "No one is saying making money isn't important. However, making money is the result of having a fulfilling workplace and bringing value to society. Making money allows you to keep living that purpose. I'm not saying money isn't important. I'm just saying it needs to be about more than money."

When a company is going through a tough time, it's easy to forget about purpose and your impact on society or your employees. It's easier to focus instead on the bottom line. "What do we need to do to make more money now?" That's when a company needs to be reminded of the importance of having a great workplace and a conscience about its value to society.

In quarterly meetings with all of my clients, we review all three characteristics of a great company.

- Are we meeting our top- and bottom-line goals?

- Are we a place where employees feel fulfilled and grow? How do we know?

- Are we adding value to society? How do we know?

If your organization is falling short on any one of these three characteristics, you must look to your leadership team.

- Are each of your leaders mastering self-leadership? Are they consistently at their best and managing their own emotions?

- Is your leadership team structured for success? Are functional accountabilities understood and changing with the needs of the business?

- When bringing new members onto your leadership team, are they all A-players?

- Is the culture of our leadership team aligned around values, vision, and vulnerability?

- Is your leadership team executing with discipline every day? Are you aligned around a small number of priorities and measures? Is there a consistent, effective planning and communication rhythm?

- Is your leadership team effectively learning and growing each and every quarter? Are there any B- and C-players on the leadership team?

To help you find opportunities to improve your leadership team,

I suggest having your entire leadership team read this book. I would then have each leader take the Breakthrough Leadership Team Assessment discussed next.

TAKE THE BREAKTHROUGH LEADERSHIP TEAM ASSESSMENT

Another critical way to measure your progress is to use the Breakthrough Leadership Team Assessment. This assessment has thirty questions in six categories and will help you and your leadership team understand how well you're exhibiting the most important characteristics of a Breakthrough Leadership Team. Your leadership team can take the assessment for free at BreakThroughLeadershipTeam.com. It should be retaken quarterly to measure progress and to identify new opportunities and challenges. Since your leadership team is the heart and soul of your company, think of this as your quarterly checkup.

This should not be an anonymous survey. The people on your leadership team must be strong enough, and feel safe enough, to give honest feedback about the team. In fact, if people balk at publicly answering questions or don't answer the questions honestly, that's a sign that you have a trust problem on the team. When this happens, it's time for the CEO to look in the mirror and ask, *What have I done to create an environment where people don't feel comfortable being open and honest? How can I change that?* At this point, go back to Chapter 4 ("Defining the Right Culture") and define a handful of action steps you can take to foster a more vulnerable culture.

BREAKTHROUGH LEADERSHIP TEAM ASSESSMENT

Rate each statement on a scale of 1 (strongly disagree) to 5 (strongly agree) based on your level of agreement:

1. Self-Leadership

____ I am continuously learning and improving.

____ I understand and leverage my strengths every day.

____ I am aware of my emotional state and have the ability to effectively manage it.

____ I focus on those things I control and accept the things I can't.

____ When I need help, I am comfortable asking for it.

2. Structuring Your Leadership Team

____ Our leadership team is structured so that each major function has one person accountable, and no member of the leadership team is stretched too thin.

____ Our leadership team has a twelve-quarter forecast for the business that drives proactive decisions regarding additions and changes to the leadership team structure.

____ Each leadership team role has a job scorecard that includes the mission, responsibilities, measures of success, and competencies required for the role.

____ Each member of the leadership team is part of a mastermind group of peers that help challenge them and act as a sounding board.

____ We have a professional services A-Team consisting of exceptional attorneys, accountants, coaches, bankers, and other critical external services.

3. Finding the Right People

____ We proactively build a virtual bench of potential A-players for the leadership team and the leadership team's direct reports.

____ We have an effective process to develop strong leaders to fill new leadership team needs from within the organization.

____ We have an effective employee referral program that generates at least one-third of our candidates for leadership positions and their direct reports.

____ We have a thorough screening, interviewing, and evaluation process that ensures 90 percent of leadership team hires are A-players.

____ Every leadership team member has a strong #2 who has the potential to be their successor.

4. Defining the Right Culture

_____ Our leadership team has developed, communicated, and lives by a set of core values that anchors our culture and is nonnegotiable.

_____ Each member of the leadership team rallies behind an inspiring core purpose that answers the question, Why does our company exist?

_____ Each leadership team member is a true believer and evangelist for our company's long-term (ten years or more) and midterm (three-year) vision.

_____ Our leadership team is a safe place for us to be honest and vulnerable, to freely admit mistakes, to ask for help, and to ask for forgiveness.

_____ Members of the leadership team consistently hold themselves and others on the team accountable for their commitments.

5. Executing with Discipline

_____ Our leadership team is aligned around no more than five priorities for the year and the quarter.

_____ There is clear accountability for each annual and quarterly priority.

_____ We measure and hold each leader accountable to two to three leading and lagging key performance indicators.

____ Our planning and communication rhythm allows us to effectively plan and adjust throughout the year and quarter to take advantage of opportunities and attack major challenges.

____ Our planning and communication rhythm drives effective communication across the leadership team and cascades down from and up to the leadership team.

6. Developing and Improving the Team

____ As a leadership team, we spend time each quarter learning and growing together (books, conferences, new tools, techniques, etc.).

____ All leadership team members are held accountable to their own learning and development plans (personal and professional).

____ All leadership team members are held accountable for ensuring their direct reports have learning and development plans (personal and professional).

____ Our leadership team assesses the talent of their direct reports quarterly and defines ninety-day action steps (coaching, mentoring, challenging, warning, etc.) for each direct report.

____ Our leadership team holds one another accountable for maximizing their team's talent as well as making the tough decision to "cut the cord" where necessary.

Note: your total score for all thirty questions is not important. The focus of this assessment is to answer three questions:

What is our highest priority, and what are the highest impact opportunities for improvement?

Where are we strongest as a leadership team, and how can we best maintain and leverage that strength?

Where do we have misalignment (large variations in scoring) across the leadership team, and what is the reason behind that misalignment?

The actual score on your Breakthrough Leadership Team Assessment is less important than your progress over time. That's why I recommend taking this assessment quarterly and reviewing your trends, up or down, over time. You will never get to some magical point where you score 5s on every question. However, you should strive for consistent improvement. Keep in mind, however, that a downward trend on a score may not always mean your team has taken a step backwards. It could also mean that your standards are changing and that you now expect more from each other. That's part of the growth process toward a Breakthrough Leadership Team.

PRIORITIZE

Once you've measured where you are on the journey to

becoming a Breakthrough Leadership Team, decide, as a leadership team, on the most impactful two to three key actions you will take over the next ninety days. If not having enough A-players is your challenge, you might commit to creating a virtual bench or starting a quarterly talent assessment process. If you have employee retention and morale issues, you might commit to defining a set of core values and a core purpose that the organization can rally around. If discipline and accountability is the challenge, you might commit to implementing the planning and communication rhythm and developing a KPI dashboard.

The key is to hold back from trying to fix all of your problems and attack all of your new opportunities all at once. No organization has the bandwidth or patience to attack so many things at one time and still keep the day-to-day business going. Take a more incremental approach, learning and adjusting as you move forward.

A NOTE TO CEOS

Leadership team improvements must be owned by you, the CEO. That doesn't mean you are responsible for implementing all of the changes. But it does mean you must be accountable and be the champion for the overall progress of your Breakthrough Leadership Team. So, as a special note to you, based on my experience and my interviews with CEOs, here are the most common mistakes CEOs make:

- **Keeping underperformers on the leadership team too long.** Remember, every person on your leadership team must be an A-player or a B-player with the potential to quickly become an A-player. B- and C-players affect every A-player on your team. They don't follow through on their commitments and they often don't embody the organization's core values. Keeping these folks around not only hurts your bottom line but also your credibility as a CEO.

- **Promoting based on longevity.** Just because someone has worked for you a long time doesn't entitle them to a seat at the leadership table. They still have to be A-players. Allowing mediocre, veteran employees on the leadership team will never allow your team to reach the next level.

- **Assuming everyone shares the company vision.** As the CEO, you may have a crystal clear vision for the company, but your team may not. They need to be constantly reminded. You need to communicate, communicate, and communicate that vision. You can't say it once or twice at a retreat and think everyone understands. You need to communicate the vision so often that people around the table roll their eyes and mouth the words as you say them. At that point, you might think you've overcommunicated. But, in fact, that's the point where people might be starting to understand what you've been saying.

- **Trying to reach a consensus.** While it's crucial for each member of the leadership team to be heard, waiting for consensus will slow things down to a crawl. Waiting for consensus in a company that wants to grow, provide opportunities, and do great things for society is death for that company. Once everyone has said their piece, the person accountable for that decision (not necessarily you) has to have the courage to make a decision and execute. A good decision executed well will get you light-years farther than a never-ending debate waiting for that magical "best decision."

- **Trying to tackle too much at once.** When I ask some CEOs what their priorities for the year or quarter are, they'll list out fifteen things. There are so many opportunities and so much that needs to be fixed that they want to do it all right away. By doing this, you're confusing and overwhelming your team. It's time to make some hard decisions about what you're saying yes and no to. If everything is a priority, nothing is a priority.

- **Inviting too many people onto the leadership team.** Some CEOs think inviting twelve or fourteen people to a planning retreat is a good way to help employees understand the vision and take ownership. That sounds logical. The reality, though, is that everyone in the room wants to have their say, so ten-minute conversations become hour-long conversations. Furthermore, with the leaders and their direct reports all in the room, there are some topics the group can't discuss. For instance, you may be having big problems with the sales division, but you can't really discuss it because the people who are the problem are sitting there. The only people you want in the room are those who are going to add value to the discussion, take ownership of financial targets and the rocks you're creating, and participate openly and honestly in all discussions. The best leadership teams typically have five to seven people. Amazon founder Jeff Bezos follows the two-pizza rule: you should be able to feed your entire team with two large pizzas.

THE RIGHT TIME IS NOW

If your leadership team is not learning and growing, it's dying. Your competitors are planning, executing, and building great companies that people love to work for and that customers admire. If you don't get to work, you will be left behind.

Review the insights you gleaned from this book, your performance related to the three characteristics of a leadership team, and the results of the Breakthrough Leadership Team Assessment and schedule a meeting with your leadership now to prioritize and begin taking action. Don't wait for the "right time." There never is one. You'll always be too busy. There will always be something more urgent to focus on. The right time is always now.

Remember what's at stake. Is your company's status quo acceptable, or do you want to create something special? Are you okay with mediocre top- and bottom-line growth, or do you want exciting growth that provides incredible opportunities for all members of the company? Are you okay with a "good enough" work environment or do you want to create a place where everyone grows and feels fulfilled? Are you okay just being in it for the money or do you want to build a company that adds real value to society? If you've read this far, you want more, and you're ready to take action.

As you know by now, you can't read this book, take the assessment, correct your problems, and be done with it. Building and developing your Breakthrough Leadership Team is an ongoing process. The key is to make consistent progress quarter after quarter. Measure your success and continually learn, reevaluate, and adjust.

Think of this as a never-ending journey. It's a North Star; you never reach it, but it continues to guide you. You don't wake up one morning and declare, "We made it! We're a Breakthrough Leadership Team!" Success comes not from achieving perfection but from striving to improve, bit by bit, every day.

ABOUT THE AUTHOR

MIKE GOLDMAN is a nationally recognized speaker, author, and business coach. As a consultant for the last thirty years, Mike has worked with Verizon, Disney, Ralph Lauren, and dozens of other midsized and Fortune 500 companies. In 2007 he founded Performance Breakthrough, where he works with leadership teams to grow their businesses and create more fulfilling work environments. His first book, *Performance Breakthrough: The Four Secrets of Passionate Organizations,* has helped business leaders create caring, productive, and profitable organizations. Mike loves to read and travel. He and his wife have two grown children and live in New Jersey.